Pressed Flowers

and

Flower Pictures

Margaret Kennedy Scott

Pressed Flowers

and

Flower Pictures

Other books by the same author and co-written with Mary Beazley:

Making Pressed Flower Pictures

Pressed Flowers through the Seasons

ISBN 0 7134 52455

Printed and bound in
Great Britain by
Anchor Brendon
Tiptree, Essex
for the publishers

B. T. Batsford Ltd
4 Fitzhardinge Street
London
W1H 0AH

Contents

Acknowledgements

I thank the following people for their help with the creation of this book: The British Museum staff for allowing me to see Mrs Delany's 'Paper Mosaicks'; Lance Cooper for photography; and my husband for all his help.

General Introduction

How often do we look at nature programmes on television and marvel at the beauty of the flowers which the art of the camera brings to us, often so much bigger than in real life? The minute details and the intricacy of form are revealed which the naked eye cannot see. And how often do we wish that we could reproduce some of this beauty either by drawing or painting or with our own photography? Some of us can do these things, but we do not all have these talents, and though we cannot hope to compete with nature, there are other ways of making pictures which, nevertheless, can give satisfaction and a sense of achievement, by using pressed flowers, dried flowers or paper collage, all of which are described in this book.

I have already produced two books with Mary Beazley on pressed flower pictures. In this book I repeat some of the more important fundamental rules to be observed in the art of making these pictures and make no apology for doing this as these rules can be so vital to the success of the creation. As well as some of the kinds of pictures described in the earlier books, I have included several completely new ideas explored and perfected as a result of experiment over the last two years. I am sure you will find these most stimulating and fascinating. For those of you who live in flats or have no garden, and perhaps are unable to make a collection of flowers, the following pages will show you how to make interesting pictures using coloured paper. For me this is a new technique in the art of creating flower pictures which I have found most absorbing. In this different form of art you need not be restricted by the actual shapes and colours of flowers as you are when making pictures from real flowers; and whilst you can still faithfully copy from life, you can if you wish let your imagination run riot. Collages made from dried flowers are also described. This book contains instructions and designs for creating all these pictures, and when you have mastered the technique of your choice you will be able to go on to make your own designs.

1 Paper collage. An informal group of mixed flowers.

At the end of this book instructions and suggestions are included for making various kinds of greetings cards.

I

Paper Collage

1
Introduction

My interest in making pictures by using coloured pieces of paper was aroused when I heard about Mrs Delany and her flower 'mosaicks'. It seemed to me that as an alternative to using pressed or dried flowers this was a fascinating way of producing flower pictures. For a lover of flowers who has no garden and who is unable to make a collection of pressed or dried flowers or for someone who may be housebound, this could be an ideal form of creative art. It needs very little equipment and is inexpensive. Ability to draw is not necessary, although the more artistic qualities one has the easier any creative work becomes.

The only material required is coloured paper, which is very easily come by. All kinds of magazines and colour supplements are rich in coloured pictures. Brightly coloured sheets of writing paper are to be found in stationers which can be bought by the sheet, and tissue paper, crêpe paper, even face tissues and many other sorts of paper can be fashioned into flower collages.

Models for the pictures can be taken from live specimens and copied freehand, or from drawings or paintings that you may have made. If you have no books or prints of flowers, these can be borrowed from your local library. In them will be found many suitable subjects. Old prints are particularly attractive and reproductions of botanical paintings can also be adapted for use. If your artistic ability does not stretch to copying a model freehand, you can always make a tracing of the subject you have chosen and transpose it onto the background, or even use it as a template for the various coloured papers needed to make up the collage.

As you become more practised you can use a flower from one illustration, another from a different source and so on, and create your own compositions. Continuing further, make abstract designs with these and just suggest the flowers you are portraying by colour and shape. You can express yourself in larger than life size flowers or you can make small greetings cards. You can copy specimens down to the last detail or make very bold designs using only a few colour variations.

Once you start on this art you will become engrossed with it and you need never run out of material to work with or models to copy.

2
Mrs Delany and her 'paper mosaicks'

Mrs Delany was a remarkable woman who, at the advanced age of 72, started making the most exquisite studies of flowers taken from life. These were produced entirely from cut-out pieces of coloured paper which she stuck onto a black background. She was born Mary Granville in 1700, the daughter of Colonel and Mrs Bernard Granville. Her father had been at one time Lieutenant Governor of Hull and also a Member of Parliament for Fowey in Cornwall. She was well educated and had great artistic talent which was apparent even at the early age of 8 when at school she used to cut out intricate patterns of birds and flowers which she took home to be framed.

She had an eventful life but of varying fortunes, having married at the age of 17 a man who was 40 years her senior. The marriage was not a success; seven years later she became a widow and remained so for 19 years. During this time she led an interesting life amongst cultured and aristocratic friends and relations. At the age of 43 Mary married again and this time her marriage was extremely happy. While staying in Ireland some years before she had met Dr Delany, an Irish protestant clergyman with a deanery near Dublin, and after the death of his second wife they married. The next 25 years were spent in Ireland and these years were the happiest ones of her life. At the age of 69 Mary Delany became a widow once more. It was not until she reached her 73rd year that she began the work which became famous amongst her large circle of friends, including royalty and the leading botanists of the day. She became engrossed in this new form of art because she had grown tired of her painting and embroidery, her cut paper and other crafts which she excelled at, and the gap left by the loss of her husband was partly filled by this fascinating new pastime.

Mary was already an expert embroideress. Amongst many works she designed and embroidered her courtdress which was covered with over two hundred different flowers, demonstrating her knowledge and love of flowers. When she started making her cut paper flowers, in ten years she created a collection of nearly one thousand pictures of plants made from paper. Sometimes she used hundreds of pieces to complete one plant and she always cut from life by eye. It must have been difficult to obtain the kind of paper she needed for this work but by this time she had returned to London where she obtained paper from sailors who had brought it from China or from 'paper stainers whose colours had run', the paper presumably then being of no use to them. George III and Queen Charlotte were greatly interested in Mrs Delany's 'Flower Mosaicks' as

she called them, her collection of which she referred to as her 'Herbal' or 'Hortus siccus' (dry garden). This was the beginning of a friendship with the royal family which lasted the rest of her life. Many flowers were brought to her to copy from the Royal Botanic Gardens at Kew and from the Chelsea Physic Garden, possibly at the suggestion of the King and Queen.

This, then, is a very brief account of Mrs Delany's life which inspired me to attempt to make flower pictures in the manner of Mrs Delany. One of her descendants, Ruth Hayden, has written a charming biography of this fascinating lady, *Mrs Delany, her life and her flowers*, from which I have extracted a few details of her remarkable life. Her paper mosaicks are housed in the Print Room at the British Museum and can be viewed on request. I recommend a visit there to anyone contemplating making paper flower collages.

Mrs Delany's flowers as well as being copied from life were also life size and were a true representation of the plants she was portraying. Some she sent as pictures to friends but most were stored in albums. In much the same way, young Victorian ladies in later years picked and pressed flowers, many of which were beautifully mounted and annotated.

It is surprising that there appear to be no collections of flower collages other than this one made some 200 years ago. It also seems, reading Mrs Delany's biography, that though she made sketches of landscapes and portraits, there are no flower paintings by her. Perhaps she preferred the challenge of paper and scissors.

It is very much easier for us to set about making collages than it was in Mary Delany's time. All kinds of paper can now be obtained in any colour, shade or texture and getting card or paper for backgrounds creates no problem. Mrs Delany's work is mounted on background paper which her biographer tells us she obtained from a paper-mill in Hampshire. This she prepared with a wash of Indian ink. Unlike Mrs Delany, we have a wide choice of ready-made adhesives whereas the glues she used were probably of flour and water or egg-white, which of course she had to make herself.

II

Making Collages

3
Preparation

Most of the paper collages illustrated in this book have been made from the colour supplements of the Sunday papers and magazines. It is only when one begins to thumb through these possible sources of material with collage in mind that one notices how many different colours and shades there are.

When you start your preparation gather together a collection of different coloured papers and store the cut pieces neatly in files by colours. If you do not do this you will find yourself frantically searching through the supplements or magazines for a colour you require and you will end up surrounded by a medley of coloured scraps of paper. Be methodical and divide your colours.

Have six files: one for reds, one for yellows to orange, another for pinks to purple, one for blues, one for greens and the sixth one for miscellaneous colours such as cream, brown and black. If you have the patience, cut off the irrelevant pieces of the page so that you are left with just the colour and not all the print which accompanies it. This may be tedious but a little care at this stage will save you a great deal of searching around later on. Then, when you are ready to make a flower you will easily be able to pick out, as though you were preparing a palette of paints, the colours you require for the particular job in hand.

You will, for example, find yourself cutting out pictures of dark red saucepans or the navy

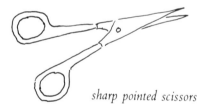

sharp pointed scissors

a soft brush

a good pair of tweezers

adhesive with nozzle

2 Essential equipment.

blue roof of a car because these are colours which might be suitable. I am not suggesting that you cut out a whole mass of coloured paper, but make a small collection which can be added to as it becomes necessary and as you find colours or shades you have not already got. Coloured writing paper is another source, and tissue paper, though liable to fade, can safely be used for shading and softening outlines.

Equipment

- Folders of coloured paper
- Paper or card on which to make the picture
- Card or hardboard for mounting
- A pair of small, sharp, pointed scissors
- A bigger pair of scissors for less delicate cutting
- Small artist's paint brush
- Adhesive. Stick 'n Fix by Bostic, Gloy or any adhesive which dries transparent and is water solvent for the sake of your paint brush
- A small cup for water — an egg-cup will do. This is useful for immersing the paint brush every so often while working, to prevent it drying and becoming hard
- A lid (jam jar top) for holding the adhesive
- A soft cloth or tissue for mopping up if the glue laps over any edges
- A soft pencil B1, 2, 3 or 4
- An India rubber
- Paper for drawing the design
- Tweezers

It is essential that you familiarize yourself with using tweezers as they will play an important part in creating the flowers you are going to make. When closed they must meet tightly so that you can pick up very small pieces of paper, such as those depicting an anther or the stem of a stamen or a tendril. You must learn to use them as an extra pair of fingers — in fact they are more efficient for fine work than your own fingers. Keep your tweezers specially for this work. If you have to buy a pair, make sure that when closed and held up to the light they close tightly. I use a pair which are 8.5 cm (3½ in.) long.

4
Tips and mountings

Unlike pressed flower pictures, which look more effective when arranged in groups of mixed flowers, paper collage flowers can very happily stand alone as single specimens. These can be copied in two different ways. First from the actual flower, which you will probably already have sketched to reduce it from three to two dimensions; secondly, you can pull the flower of your choice apart and reproduce it piece by piece. To make as accurate a copy as possible you should find the appropriate colours in at least a range of light, medium and dark shades. A single page of a colour supplement will often provide a sufficient mixture of colours to produce the various shades you need. Remember that as the artist all you

have to do is to make your interpretation of the model you are copying in the same way as a painter would reproduce the model in front of him. Secondly, there are many books containing prints of flowers and plants, and gardening books and seed catalogues yield good copy. Find a fairly simple subject, such as the *Paeonia clusii* (fig. 16), which was taken from a book on botanical art, and work on that.

There follow some general notes which you will find helpful in putting your collage pictures together and after the notes examples of six pictures I have made are given with illustrations and detailed instructions on how they can be

poppy

tulip

pansies

auriculas

3 Easy flower shapes to sketch.

copied if you should prefer first to experiment in this way before embarking on your own.

Tracing

Unless you are sure of your ability to place accurately the paper shapes which will make up the design you have chosen you should lightly draw in the outline of the design, using a soft pencil. If you are unable to do this freehand use tracing paper. Place this on whatever you wish to copy and, with a soft pencil, draw the outline. If the subject is complicated, simplify it by leaving out much of the detail — you can always add more later. Remove the tracing paper, turn it over and with a very soft pencil (3 or 4B) rub over all the lines you have drawn. Turn the paper face upwards again and, placing it on the background card or paper you will be using and securing it with clips to make sure it will not move, redraw along your original lines. This will mark your background sufficiently, if it is of a light colour, to show you the outlines. If the background is dark rub the reverse of the tracing paper with a white pastel stick.

Gluing

In most cases the adhesive is applied onto the reverse side of the petal, leaf or stem or of whatever else you are making. However, when arranging petals which meet in the centre, place a spot of adhesive at that point on the background, smearing it to make a small circle about 1 cm (½ in.) in diameter, and place the centre points of the petals on this. You will be able to stick them down more firmly later on, if necessary. At all times use as small a quantity of adhesive as possible. Always have a small cloth or tissue handy to mop up any adhesive that laps over the edges.

Tweezers

Always use tweezers for picking up material.

Finishing

In order to ensure that all the material used in your picture is firmly stuck down lift up any loose shapes and gently brush a thin layer of adhesive underneath them. Allow the finished collage time to adhere thoroughly to the background by leaving it for at least an hour covered with a clean piece of paper and weighed down with a heavy book.

Before framing remove all pencil marks with a soft rubber.

Although the same method of framing collages is used as for pressed flower pictures (see p. 59), the same care does not have to be exercised in handling them before the frames are nailed down as the material is fixed and so there is no risk of anything slipping.

4 *Composition of a lily.*

Frames and mounts

Paper collages seem to sit more comfortably in modern type frames, and mounts further enhance the finished work. Narrow frames nearly always need mounts, which most art shops and galleries nowadays supply. It is possible to buy them ready-cut to fit the average size frames, or they can be cut to order in a large variety of colours. It is also quite easy to buy mounting board, or the slightly thinner card, and to make your own mounts. Unless you are very clever you will not achieve the sloping angle that the professionally-produced mounts have, but with a sharp knife you will be able to cut a very satisfactory mount. Buy a small Stanley knife which has a razor-sharp blade (Stanley knife 10-601). It is very inexpensive and can be obtained from any DIY shop. Cut on a piece of board otherwise you will slice into the surface on which you are working. Measure carefully and with a ruler as a guide and holding it very firmly run the knife along the edge of the ruler. With this knife you should be able to make a clean cut. The mount can be finished by drawing lines round the inner edges in any colour you choose.

Small pictures on card, say 15 cm x 10 cm (6 in. x 4 in.), can be made without mounts but can be finished with a line or lines drawn round the edge, or made on a smaller piece of paper than the background card and mounted in this way.

a

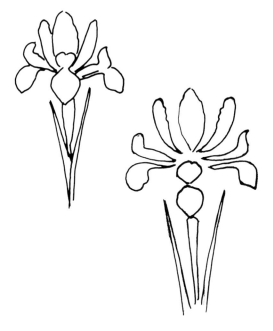

5 *Composition of an iris.*

Double mounts

It is also possible to pick out the colour of the flowers or leaves and double mount the finished picture, using colours to tone with the arrangement. Assuming the picture you are making is to go into a small frame measuring 20 cm x 15 cm (8 in. x 6 in.), cut your card to fit that size. To make the border cut a rectangle of contrasting coloured paper or thin card 15 cm x 11 cm (6 in. x 4½ in.). Stick this onto the background taking care that it is equidistant from the edges. The actual picture is then mounted on a background measuring 13 cm x 8.5 cm (5 in. x 3½ in.). This will leave a second border of contrasting colour of approximately 1 cm (½ in.). Lines can be drawn round the edges of the mount and background to make a neat finish to the arrangement.

There are numerous coloured pens you can buy for drawing lines including gold and silver, or you can use a fibre-tipped pen for this purpose.

b

6 *Double mounts: (a) a wide border picks out one of the colours of the flowers; (b) a narrow contrasting edge makes a double mount.*

Colour

Most of the flowers in the pictures which are described in the following pages have been simplified by making use of just three shades of a colour — light, medium and dark shades. In some cases, however, in order to obtain the desired effect or because there is such a wide variety of shades of colour to be found in some of the flowers, a fourth or fifth shade has been introduced.

With only three shades of a colour I have still found a good result can be achieved if the middle shade is adopted as the basic colour and the highlights are brought out in the lighter shade and the shadows in the darker shade. Where, for instance, there are five gradations in colour the range would be very light, light, medium, (being the basic colour), dark and very dark.

In the picture of the paeony, for example, (colour pl. 2) six different shades of green have been used, but the purpose of this was rather to show the natural variations in colour of the individual leaves than to bring out highlights and shadows. In the case of the geranium (p. 29) the four different greens used on the other hand depict light and shade, whilst the petals of the chrysanthemums in *Flowers in a Basket* (p. 22) have been cut from lemon, yellow and orange colours simply for effect.

5
Making simple flowers

Before you start on your first picture, make one or two single flowers to give yourself the feel of the medium you are working in. Taking a piece of card or paper as a background about 20 cm x 15 cm (8 in. x 6 in.), figs 7 and 8 show you how to put together three simple flowers using the minimum of material and only a few variations in colour. Always remember that no two petals in the real thing are exactly the same.

A daisy (fig. 7)

Materials — coloured paper
Petals — white or near white
Centres — yellow or pale green
Stems — green

a

placing the petals

7 Making a daisy.

b

completed flower

the shape of centre

1 Cut 15 petals using white or near white paper. Two different whites can be used if you wish.

2 Cut an oval shape for the centre in a yellow or pale green colour with a semi-circle of darker green or yellow for the shading. Without this you will have a very flat daisy.

3 Cut a slightly curved piece of green paper for the stem.

4 Squeeze onto your jam pot lid a small drop of adhesive.

5 Place a dab of adhesive on the centre spot where the petals will meet, and with your finger smear a circle 1 cm (½ in.) in diameter.

6 Place a petal onto the centre and continue with all the petals in the same way. By using adhesive only on one end of the petals, if you need to alter the position of any of them, this can easily be done without causing harm to the rest of the material or, if done quickly, to the petals themselves (a).

7 Having arranged the petals, you can then cover their points with the oval centre. Before adding the adhesive decide exactly where to put the centre (b). Paint the centre with adhesive and stick in place, then add the darker piece of yellow or green paper to provide shading.

8 Finally, lift up a petal and insert the top of the stem underneath.

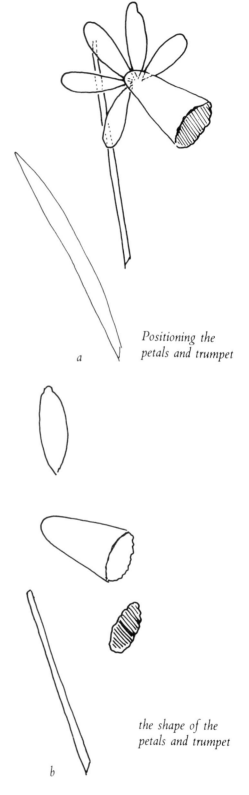

Positioning the petals and trumpet

a

A daffodil (fig. 8)

Materials	— coloured paper
Flower	— pale yellow, deep yellow, orange
Stems and leaves	— pale green, darker green

1 Cut five petals of pale yellow, one trumpet of deep yellow and one oval shape of orange for the inside of the trumpet (a).

2 Paint the adhesive on the pointed ends of the petals and place in position.

3 Brush adhesive onto top and bottom of trumpet and place on petals (b).

4 Cover the orange oval with adhesive and stick onto the trumpet.

the shape of the petals and trumpet

b

8 Making a daffodil.

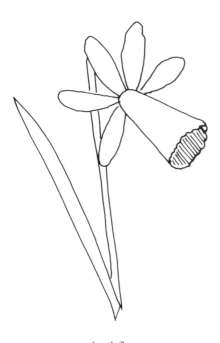

completed flower

5 Place the stem in position, lifting petals to insert stem underneath.
6 Add leaf.

A tulip (fig. 9)

This is a bi-coloured tulip.

Materials	— coloured paper
Petals	— basic colour cream
Stripes	— medium red
Underside	— dark red
of petals	
Stem	— light green
Leaf	— light green, medium green

1 Cut six cream petals using the shapes in fig. 9a as a guide.
2 Cut thirteen medium red coloured stripes.
3 Cut two dark red pieces.
4 Stick the stripes onto the petals (a).
5 Smear adhesive where the base of the flower will be.
6 Stick the petals down in the correct order (*fig. 9b*) and add the two undersides of the petals.
7 Cut out the stem and add to the base of the tulip.
8 Cut two shades for the leaf, using the darker shade for the part which is turned over.

If you like you could add more stripes to the tulip, perhaps using another shade of red.

6
Design for pictures

Poppies I (fig. 10)

This simple design is a good one to start with and would, for example, be suitable for a child's room. The poppies, dog daisies and buttercups have been cut with the minimum of detail sufficient to leave no doubt as to what they are meant to represent. The picture portrays a cornfield. In the foreground are two poppies with black centres and further shapes have been cut to resemble more poppies in the grass in the background. The edges of four circles of white paper have been serrated to represent daisies. For these, thin typing paper was used and one daisy has been folded in half to give a profile view. Long and short strips of varying greens have been added as stems and grasses, and the only concession to detail are the sharply cut grass heads. Three bright yellow buttercups dominate the centre foreground. The arrangement is mounted on green card in a very simple white wooden frame. The whole measures 43 cm x 25cm (17 in. x 10 in.).

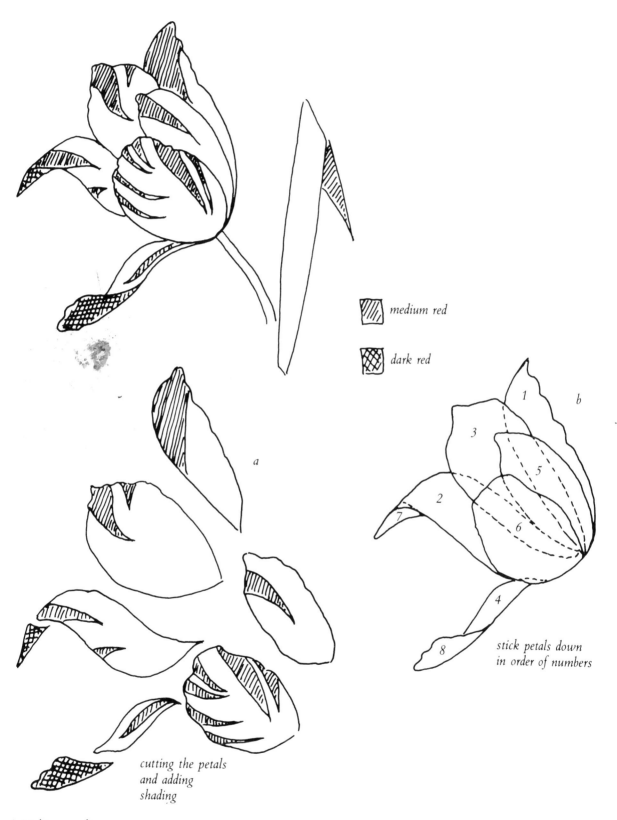

medium red

dark red

a

b

1

3

5

2

7

6

4

8

stick petals down
in order of numbers

cutting the petals
and adding
shading

9 Making a tulip.

10 Paper collage used to make a colourful arrangement of poppies and daisies in a field. A white wooden frame complements the daisies.

Method (fig. 11)

1 Cut eight petals in three different shades of red (a).
2 Cut 15 shapes in shades of red for the smaller flowers, making some of tissue paper to give the effect of poppies at a distance. See completed picture.
3 Stick all these in place.
4 Using a variety of greens, cut several pieces of grass in different lengths and widths. Add to picture.
5 Cut four circles in white for the daisies (b). Nick round the edges. Fold one over. Add three oval centres cut in green, red and yellow and one sepal in green for the folded flower.
6 Using bright yellow cut the buttercup petals, three large petals for the flower at the top of the picture and ten smaller petals for the two remaining flowers. The facing flower has a green centre. One buttercup needs a green sepal. Stick all three flowers in position (c).
7 Cut two serrated shapes to represent the poppy leaves (d).
8 Cut six grass heads in green and pale brown, sharply indent them and add them to the picture together with any more grasses you feel are needed.

11 Poppies I. Making the picture.

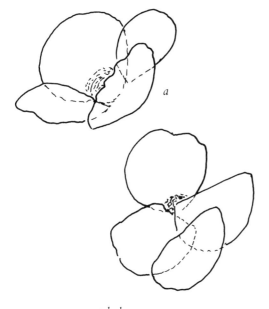

petal shapes

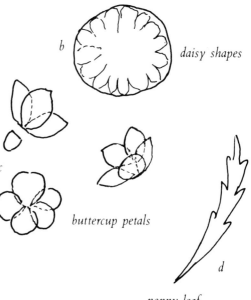

daisy shapes

buttercup petals

poppy leaf

Poppies II (fig. 12)

The second design is more detailed than the first. The picture is much bigger, the frame measuring 43 cm x 30 cm (21 in. x 12 in.). The picture itself is on a white card 43 cm x 20 cm (17 in. x 8 in.) mounted on a black background, the whole being framed in a plain narrow black moulding. The poppies are a little larger than life size and four different reds have been used in their creation. The leaves have been carefully cut from three different greens. A poppy seed head and two buds are included in the picture and the bottom foreground is finished with several blades of grass. This is a simple but very effective and pleasing arrangement and is not difficult to copy.

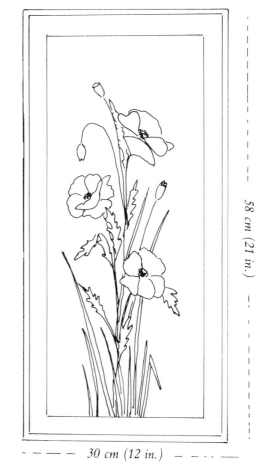

12 Poppies II. Four shades of red make up the colours of these field poppies, which are slightly larger than life size.

13 The finished design.

Method

See fig. 14 for positioning of material.

1 Poppy 1. Cut three petals of mid-red, one of dark red, two of very dark red (a) (b) (c). Poppy 2. Cut three petals of mid-red, two of dark red and one of very dark red (d) (e) (f). Poppy 3. Cut three petals of mid-red and two of dark red (g) (h) (i).

2 Tear three circles of black paper for the centres.

3 Stick the three poppies in place, inserting the centres at the same time.

4 Cut five leaves using three different greens with the lightest leaf at the top (j).

5 Cut the stems using mid-green. Make a sharp curve for the drooping bud. Cut and add the two buds and the seed head.

6 Cut nine blades of grass in different widths and lengths and in the three greens. The longer ones are inserted behind the petals of the lower poppy.

very light red

medium red

dark red

very dark red

red tissue paper

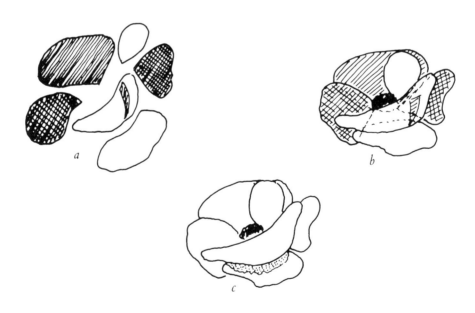

a

b

c

Poppy 1

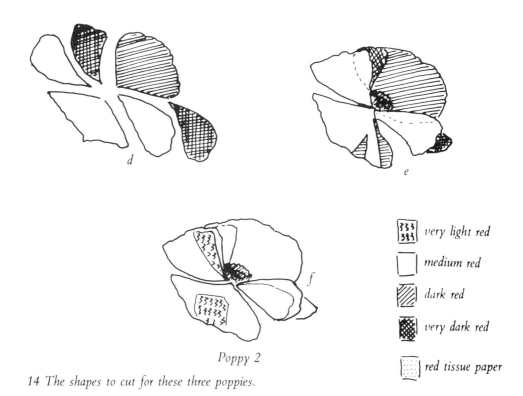

Poppy 2

| very light red |
| medium red |
| dark red |
| very dark red |
| red tissue paper |

14 The shapes to cut for these three poppies.

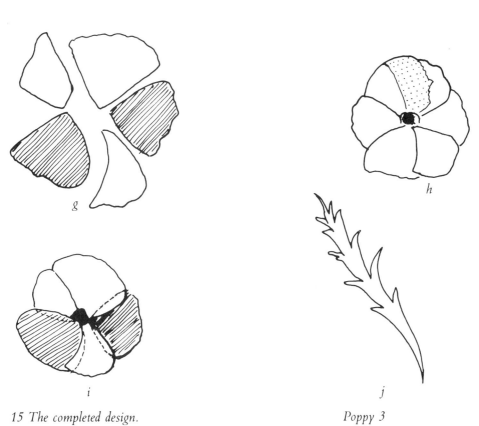

15 The completed design.

Poppy 3

16 Making a paeony: (a) petals of white paper with white tissue paper added; (b) leaves of differing shapes and sizes; (c) grey shadows added to the petals; (d) stamens added; (e) the flower completed; (f) (g) (h) constructions of the bud.

white tissue paper

pale grey paper

Paeony (fig. 16)

This reproduction of *Paeonia clusii* was simplified considerably for collage. The number of leaves was reduced from 94 to 59. There is no shading on the individual leaves but at least six different shades of green have been used to give this effect, the shades ranging from very light yellow to dark olive green. The stems are of deep crimson, as is the bud with green sepals, and a glimpse of white shows where a petal is just breaking through. The flower itself is made of ordinary white paper with palest grey shading and pieces of white tissue paper have been added to give a different texture. The stamens are composed of very fine strips of orange and yellow tissue paper covering the crimson stigma. The whole arrangement is very simple and a recognizable representation of the original print with the actual flower measuring 9 cm x 6 cm (3½ in. x 2½ in.). The background is of fawn card and measures 35 cm x 25.5 cm (14 in. x 10 in.).

17 Paeoni clusi.

Method (fig . 17)

1 Cut six petals in white paper (a) and cut 'shadows' of white tissue paper and stick to the petals (a).
2. Cut the narrow pointed leaves using varied greens. Cut some curved and others straight and in differing sizes (b).
3 Cut grey 'shadows' and add these (b).
4 Make a small circle of adhesive on the background where the petals will meet and stick the three upper ones in place.
5 Cut fine strips of orange and yellow tissue paper for the stamens and two larger pieces of crimson tissue paper for the centre. Stick these onto the three petals already in place (c).
6 Add the remaining petals (d).
7 Cut stems of crimson tissue paper and stick down.
8 Place the darkest leaves at the back of the arrangement — use the finished drawing as a guide.
9 Add the bud last; (f) (g) (h) show how it is constructed.

Geranium in a mount (fig. 18)

This picture of a single stem of geranium has been taken from a water colour I recently painted. It is

18 (Right) Paper collage is used to make the geranium larger than life.

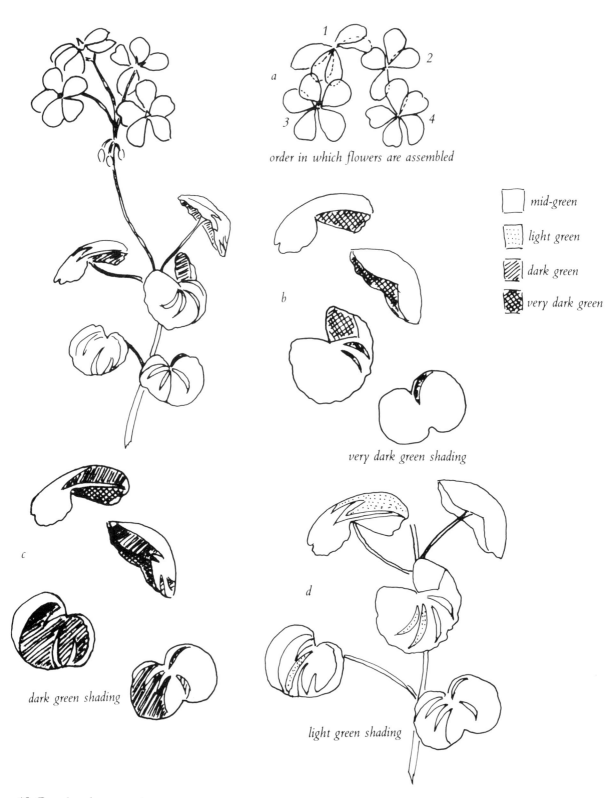

order in which flowers are assembled

mid-green

light green

dark green

very dark green

very dark green shading

dark green shading

light green shading

19 Geranium in a mount.

on a white background in a green mount in a modern gilt frame. It was a rewarding picture to make, the red of the flowers and the bright green of the leaves showing up well on the white ground. Five different shades of red were used for the flowers and four of green for the leaves. The geranium is life size measuring 23 cm (9 in.), the frame is 35 cm x 25.5 cm (14 in. x 10 in.), and the mount, 25.5 cm x 15 cm (10 in. x 6 in.).

Method (fig. 19)

1 Cut 19 mixed red petals and arrange in position (a).
2 Cut the stems and insert them under the petals by gently lifting the petals and brushing a little adhesive onto the undersides.
3 Cut the main stem with strips for shading and five leaves in the mid-green shade and stick all in position. Use the drawing as a guide (b).
4 To finish the leaves, (c) and (d) show the order in which they should be built up. Very dark green shapes should be cut out and stuck onto the mid-green as illustrated, followed by the light green shapes where needed and finally by the very light green shapes as shown.

20 *The convolvulus,* Ipomoea rubro-caerulea, *is taken from a book of botanical pictures.*

5 Cut three buds and short curved stems, sepals for the back of one flower and centres for the other three. Stick all these in place.

Convolvulus (fig. 20)

This is an interesting and not too complicated picture to make, which I set in a gilt frame on a dark green mount. The frame measures 31 cm x 25.5 cm (12½ in. x 10 in.) and the space inside the mount 20 cm x 15 cm (8 in. x 6 in.). The background is of white cartridge paper. Four different shades of blue make up the two convolvulus flowers, very dark, dark, medium and light and three different shades of green for the leaf and tendrils.

Method (fig. 21)

First using a soft pencil, lightly draw the outline of the flowers onto the background. To make sure the positioning is correct try the mount and frame on top.

1 For the main flower cut five petals of medium blue paper (a).
2 Stick light blue pieces onto the petals. One of the petals turns back with a very dark blue shadow under the fold; (b) shows how this is composed.
3 Smear a small drop of adhesive where the centre of the flower is to be and arrange the petals in position.
4 Add five strips of dark blue to mark the indentations of the petals (a).
5 Fill the centre with a 'star' of very dark blue cut into seven fine points (c).
6 Indicate the stamens by three thin strips of light blue.
7 The flower in profile (d) has five petals, two very dark blue, one dark blue and two of medium blue. Stick the very dark shapes first, one being the petal behind, which is just visible.
8 Cut the leaf using the dark green paper (e). The medium and light shades are used for shadows and to suggest veins. Do not stick the leaf down finally until the stem is in position.
9 Cut curving strips of medium green for the upper sections of the stem, with a thicker strip for the part which emerges from under the leaf at the base of the picture.

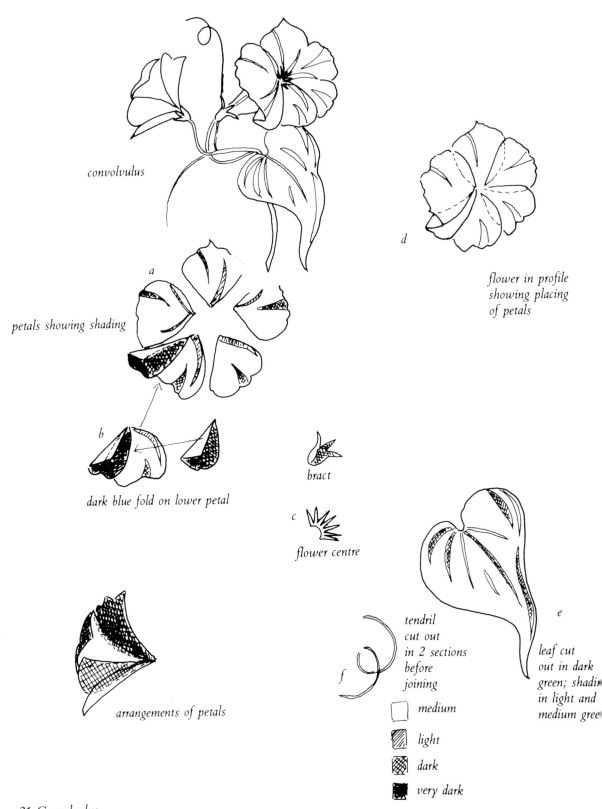

convolvulus

petals showing shading

a

b

dark blue fold on lower petal

bract

c

flower centre

d

*flower in profile
showing placing
of petals*

arrangements of petals

*tendril
cut out
in 2 sections
before
joining*

f

medium

light

dark

very dark

e

*leaf cut
out in dark
green; shadi[ng]
in light and
medium gree[n]*

21 Convolvulus.

10 Cut some very fine strips of dark and light green as shadows and highlights on the stem.

11 Cut two sharp angled curves and join them together to make the upper tendril (f). It is easier to cut it in two pieces than to try and cut something as fine in one piece. Cut the lower tendril. Stick both in position.

12 The sepals are added last. These are dark green with a highlight of medium green (g).

13 Add more adhesive where necessary to ensure all the pieces stay in place.

Flowers in a basket (fig. 22)

This is a very free copy of a fifteenth-century Chinese painting on silk and has been given a fairly modern treatment. The picture has been put together on a background of cream card inside a plum-coloured mount in a gilt frame. The frame measures 35 cm x 29 cm (14 in. x 11½ in.) and the inside of the mount 23 cm x 16 cm (9 in. x 6½ in.). The outline of the basket and the shapes of the flowers were drawn in very lightly. Light orange-brown was used for the backing for the basket with darker strips of brown paper being woven diagonally both ways to give the effect of the wicker weave. The top of the basket was

made from a plain piece of the backing paper, with strips of a darker colour and the base cut from the same dark paper. The three large chrysanthemums were made in a mixture of orange, yellow and lemon colours. The small purple chrysanthemums on the right were cut in two shades of purple and the two pinks with jagged edges in pale mauve paper. The centres consisted of a white circle with a smaller deep purple inside it, on which was placed a yet smaller circle of off-white with a dark purple spot in the centre. The geranium on the left was made with bright vermillion with two darker petals. The rose in the centre is deep pink. Three different shaped leaves were cut out using mixed greens. The shapes of the leaves were formed in character with the flowers in the basket, linear or pointed for the pinks and the bamboo and indented for the chrysanthemums whilst narrow, oval, pointed leaves were cut for the rose.

Method (fig. 23)

1 Draw the outline of the arrangement.

2 Make up the basket before pasting onto the background of the picture. Cut the shape of the basket in light orange-brown paper.

3 Cut 26 strips of a darker shade so that they will contrast nicely with the background of the basket. Cut these in slightly different widths and a little longer than the actual size. Weave these diagonally both ways (a). It will help if a spot of adhesive is put on one end of the reverse side of each strip as you weave. This will help to prevent the strands slipping out of place. When the weaving is completed, stick the remaining ends down and trim off the overlapping pieces.

4 Stick the basket onto the background of the picture.

5 Cut narrow shaped pieces of the backing colour of the basket to stick down both sides to give it a tidy finish.

6 Cut 37 mixed petals of orange, yellow and lemon for the three chrysanthemums. Use 16 for the one on the right, 11 for the one in profile and 10 for the left hand one (b). Stick these three in place. Cut and stick the two centres and one sepal.

7 Make the pinks. Cut 10 triangular petals of lilac paper with jagged edges (c). Stick these in place with the points to the centre.

22 Flowers in a basket.

23 Making the picture: (a) weaving the basket; (b) the chrysanthemums; (c) the pinks; (d), (e), (f) the three circles for the centres of the pinks; (g), (h) the rose; (i) the shapes of the leaves; (j) the handle of the basket.

8 For the centre of the pinks, cut two white circles and one of deep purple or blue (d) (e) (f).

9 Cut 17 mixed purple petals for the two smaller chrysanthemums. Stick them in place with one centre and one sepal.

10 Cut two vermillion and three lighter red petals for the geranium and stick down with a tiny triangle of yellow for the centre.

11 Make the rose, (g) (h) and stick down.

12 Cut two stems for the flowers in profile and a stem for the bamboo shoot and stick.

13 Cut seven narrow, pointed leaves in mixed green, five of olive green with indented edges and twelve grey-green linear leaves (i). Also cut four grass-green spiky leaves for the bamboo in the centre of the arrangement. Stick these all down placing them underneath the petals where necessary.

14 Finish the basket by cutting the top out of the paler brown paper and the base out of the darker brown. Stick in place. Cut strips of dark brown paper as uprights along the top of the basket and stick.

15 Cut three strips of brown for the handle (j) —the nearest upright and the horizontal of light brown and the far upright of dark brown. Stick these down making sure the perspective of the handle is correct.

Groups of flowers (fig. 24)

Figure 24 shows three groups of flowers arranged on a black background that complements the flowers extremely well. These three groups were taken from different books and adapted to fit the design. The individual flowers have been made as simply as possible to give the required effect, with the primrose petals cut from three different cream coloured papers and three different greens used to show the shading of the leaves. The various tones of pink from which the fuchsia was made were all taken from one page of a magazine. Although the leaves have been cut as simply as possible, care must always be taken to ensure that the shape of the leaves is in character with the flower you are copying.

The petals of the pinks, which are so well defined against the black background, have been cut from just off-white and pale pinky-grey paper, which has been carefully but erratically fringed to reproduce the characteristic of this

24 *These groups of flowers show up brilliantly against a black background.*

particular dianthus, whilst the leaves and sepals are of two shades of grey-green paper found on the same page.

Daisies in a clip frame (fig. 27)

Clip frames are quite inexpensive. They come in all sizes and make a good setting for collages. These frames consist of a piece of hardboard, a piece of glass or perspex and four clips which hold the glass in place. The daisies on a black background have been set in a parchment-coloured mount round which a black line has been drawn 5 mm (¼ in.) from the inside edge. The petals of the daisies have been cut separately from strips of ordinary thin white paper and white tissue paper, with a few petals made of pink tissue paper. A small spot of adhesive was put where the petals would meet in the middle and each petal was placed so that they radiated outwards. More tissue paper petals were used in making the daisy in profile as the slight transparency of this kind of paper gives the impression that the flower is

framed

primroses

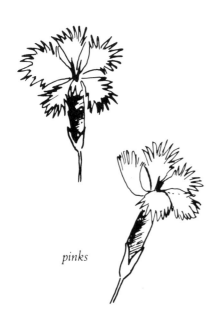

pinks

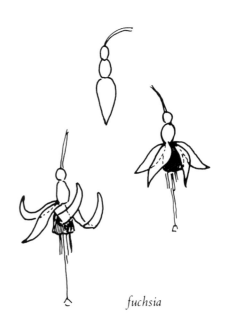

fuchsia

25 *An attractive way of presenting small groups of flowers.*

receding into the background. The four stems are slightly curved. Avoid cutting straight ones — they are never comfortable nor do they look right. The leaves fade nicely into the background by the use of very dark green, and this is emphasized by the lighter colour of the leaves in the foreground.

26 A clip frame sets off the simple daisies in paper collage on a black ground.

28 Daisies Bellis perennis.

29 Adapted from a Redouté print. This paper collage of roses is arranged on a black ground.

27 Daisies in a clip frame.

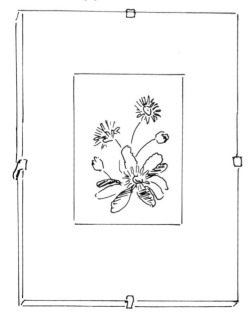

Garden flowers

The group of flowers on the jacket has been adapted from a nineteenth-century water colour in the Musée des Beaux-Arts at Lyons by the French artist Berjon. It has been greatly simplified, but the basic design remains, though for some of the flowers in the original painting I have substituted others. The painting depicts a bunch of mixed flowers which appear to have just been picked and laid down on a flat surface, waiting perhaps to be arranged later in a vase. Two large tulips dominate the top left-hand corner. Four single roses in shades of orange to red fill the centre, leading down to two different coloured violas. On the left is a rose in profile with two buds and some sharply serrated rose leaves. Two small mauve asters and a bud appear from behind the leaves at the top of the arrangement off centre on the right, with a lilac tulip a little below. Some stalks of cornflowers are arranged on the right joining the stems of the other flowers at an angle. Dark tulip leaves placed behind the arrangement give depth to the whole composition. The flowers are arranged on a faintly green background in a fairly heavy dull silver frame. The group measures approximately 32 cm (13 in.) long and 20 cm (8 in.) wide.

30 Lilies. Flowers made from cream paper and two shades of red. The leaves are three shades of green.

III

Pressed Flower Pictures

7
Introduction

I have been making pressed flower pictures now for about 20 years and all the time I have been discovering new things from which ideas develop. By experimenting I have found other flowers to press and been able to obtain different effects by using other methods of making pictures. Two or three layers of flowers may be placed one on top of the other to achieve a three-dimensional appearance. By placing the flowers differently so that they appear to be growing, a garden or border can be made. A picture can be constructed after the style of the Dutch flower painters by arranging a large group with the emphasis on the bigger flowers at the top of the picture. In addition vases or containers can be simulated by using flowers or leaves or parts of flowers or leaves to hold your flowers, or you could try

31 Pressing a primrose.

making an arrangement in a mount. All these methods in their different ways will produce pleasing and effective pictures, but I must confess that my favourite pictures are the groups of flowers in what I call the Victorian style in an oval gilt frame; if you are lucky enough to find one, an antique frame, is the most attractive.

8
What to press

To make pressed flower pictures naturally enough, you must have acquired a collection of flowers and leaves which you have picked and pressed, perhaps through the summer. This does not mean that the summer is the only time for pressing — far from it — at any time of the year there is always something to press. The evergreens are always with us, the ivy, the euonymus, the mahonia or the skeleton leaves which you may find under bushes. Do remember that however carefully you press your specimens, a percentage will not be usable. A small insect that escaped your notice will by the time you open your press have been feasting on some of your carefully arranged specimens, so rendering them useless.

Others may not have been quite as fresh as you thought and so have lost a lot of their colour, though this need not always be a disadvantage as you may find a use in your picture for a flower that has acquired a faded cream or brown shade. When you remove your flower if it is brittle a petal might break or tear, so always press more than you think you will need; after all they will always come in useful for another picture. When you pick a flower to press pick some with the stems so that you can use the whole flower. Use some heads only, placing them face down or on their backs, depending on which way they lie most comfortably. You will probably have to remove the calyx. Place others in profile, leaving the flower stem on, and if possible arrange some facing three-quarters to the front. This will make a much more interesting picture than just using a 'full frontal' specimen. You can even arrange a back view; this is very effective, particularly with daisies.

Some flowers with a cluster of blooms on the stem can be pressed whole — for example, cowslips and verbena — but trim off some of the surplus blooms if they appear to be too crowded. You can always cut off more if necessary when the flower has been pressed. Snip or pull off individual flowers to press separately.

Double flowers

Double flowers can cause a slight problem — I do not recommend pressing large roses for instance, and I would never attempt to press a paeony. If you must try large flowers, press petals separately and join them later. Small floribunda, miniature and rambler roses press well, but you will probably find that you will have to remove some of the central petals with your tweezers in order to expose the stamens. If you do not do this you will get a round unidentifiable blob.

32 Small double rose with some of the centre petals removed.

Most daisies would be described as double. In fact, each flower is a head of tiny, tightly packed florets covering the central disc. Daisies are invaluable, including the common type found growing on grassland or on your lawn. The yellow and lemon anthemis and the white variety are other types of daisies very suitable for

feverfew

oxeye daisy

33 Daisy shapes.

pressing. Marigold and dronicum are two more daisy shapes, easy to obtain and easy to grow. The petals of these last two become rather transparent when dried but they develop a translucent sheen, which is attractive and can add variety and light to a picture. To give a little more depth of colour use two flowers, placing one on top of the other.

One of the most useful flowers in the daisy family, and one which I consider a must if you are a serious picture maker, is the annual everlasting xeranthemum. This has white or mauve flowers, some double and some single. If you grow them yourself, pick out the ones that are single. They press very easily; the double variety will need to have some of the centre petals removed. The colours keep well. I am particularly fond of the white ones which have a wonderful satin sheen, adding beautiful highlights to a picture. The buds are a good shape too. All double or bulky flowers will need to be pressed for longer than the thinner varieties.

hellebore

passion flower

anemone

Flowers with prominent centres

34 *Flowers with prominent centres.*

Many flowers have prominent centres, which make it difficult to press them successfully. Hellebores are an example of this, but they are such useful plants that it is worth taking some trouble over them. They flower early in the year — the 'Christmas Rose' *Helleborus niger* followed by the green varieties *H. viridis* and *H. foetidus*, and then *H. orientalis*, the lenten lily — in varying shades from pink to purple. If you have plenty try pressing some whole. The centre rarely stays in the middle, so you may end up with rather a lopsided specimen. On some of the flowers cut out the calyx, the stamen and the pistil and press them separately. You can then choose the best ones to use with your most successfully pressed flowers.

Under the same heading comes one of my favourite flowers, the passion flower, which adds distinction to any arrangement and therefore should be treated with great respect. Despite its reputation as an exotic plant, it is not difficult to grow, and once established, will flower until the frost kills the blooms. Mine flowered in its second year, and each year I have to prune it hard back. To press, cut out the stamen and the pistil, and the ovary, which is situated in the centre of the flower, and place all the parts separately in the press. You can put them together again later to re-form the flower. Be sure that the anthers are yellow, which will indicate that the flower is fresh. This applies to all flowers — if a bloom is over its first youth the pollen darkens. Incidentally the passion flower is the only one on which I sometimes have to use colouring. I do this with a felt-tipped pen to emphasise the dark on the fringe of the small hairs surrounding the centre.

Bell-shaped flowers

Bell-shaped flowers include lilies, most of which can only be pressed in profile. The bigger lily flowers can be used in a 'Dutch' flower arrangement, but most are too big for the average picture. The martagon lily, if you are lucky enough to acquire it, is an ideal size, about 3½ cm (1½ in.). The early lily *pyrenaicum* is also suitable — but be grateful for any lily to add beauty to your arrangement. Easy to obtain, the lily of the valley is a very useful and a pretty addition. Even the bluebell, which I thought would never press, does press, but like all succulent plants it will have to be moved frequently in the press to a dry spot, because the paper becomes very damp as it absorbs the moisture from the drying plant.

I have pressed many tulips, whole, bisected, single, double, big and small, with great success. The bisected halves look most effective with the anthers, stamen and pistil exposed, rather like a

43

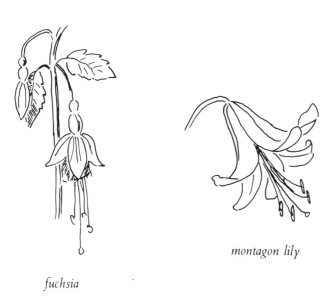

fuchsia

montagon lily

lily of the valley

35 Bell-shaped flowers.

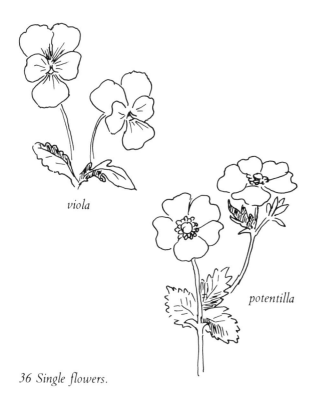

viola

potentilla

36 Single flowers.

botanical specimen. Some petals can be removed from the double blooms when dry if necessary; they can even be arranged to make the flower appear bigger and more important. The colours, too, are excellent. The red ones seem to be particularly good, and the mixed red and yellow blooms are most exciting. Even the pale pink double tulip (peach blossom) is beautiful when pressed and has a wonderful satin sheen. These are but a few that I have tried. There are many more that I am sure will give equally good results.

Flowers on spikes and sprays

Flowers on spikes and sprays are usually easy to press but need hard pressing. The freshness is indicated by the small buds at the end of the spikes. Always make sure that there are several buds which have not yet come out. If there seems to be a quantity of open flowers on the stem, pick some off. These can often be pressed individually, particularly with larkspur and delphinium. Even a lavender stem presses better for the removal of a few of the flowers. You can also tidy your specimens up when they come out of the press if you find the blossoms too congested.

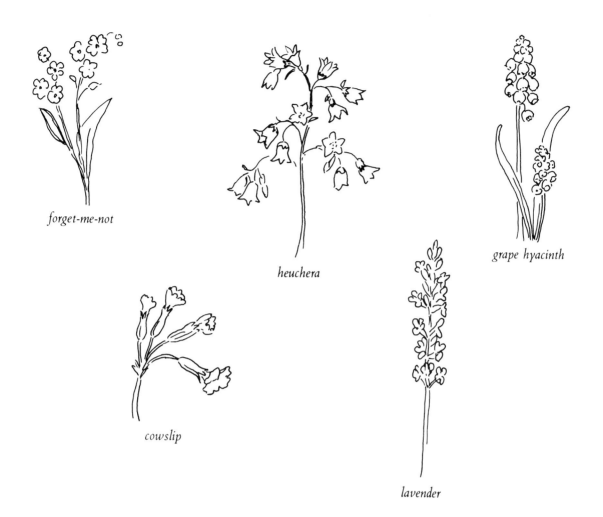

forget-me-not

heuchera

grape hyacinth

cowslip

lavender

37 Flower sprays and spikes.

Flowers in clusters

To produce an interesting picture you need variety in your material. An arrangement made entirely of single blooms would be rather dull so try and mix the shapes of your flowers. Clusters of flowers can be used whole in many cases, such as the head of the annual verbena, or the lacy head of cow parsley or a spray of cowslips. Single flowers can be picked off most of these clusters and pressed separately.

Seed heads and grasses

To add still more interesting variety to your pictures do not forget seed heads. Many being already dry will only have to be flattened. Ironing between two pieces of blotting paper will do this and so save valuable space in the press. Honesty seed pods and fluffy clematis seed heads are well

38 Flowers in clusters.

worth putting with your store of material. Poppy heads and love-in-a-mist are best picked before completely dry and pressed in the usual way.

Some grasses can be used to make straight lines in your arrangements. Many suitable varieties can be found by your taking a walk in the nearest field in summer time. Less common is the beautiful waving quaking grass and hare's tail both of which can be grown very easily from seed.

Foliage

Foliage must not be ignored; it plays a big part in the making of a picture. It can dominate or it can help to eke out a rather sparse collection of flowers. In fact fig. 46 is a picture made almost entirely of leaves. Many of the flowers you pick will have foliage that can be used as well. Different leaves have different textures; it is important to take advantage of this to add interest and variation to the arrangement. *Stachys lanata* has a velvet surface. *Alchemilla alpina* has a satin

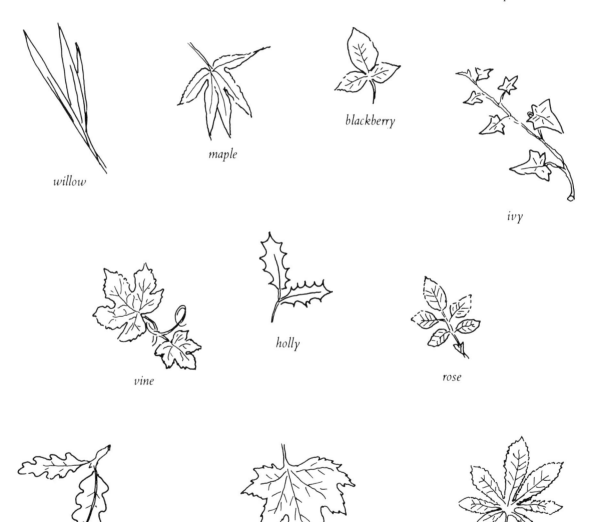

willow

maple

blackberry

ivy

vine

holly

rose

oak

sycamore

chestnut

39 Leaves.

46

40 Leaves and grasses only are used to create this picture of pressed material.

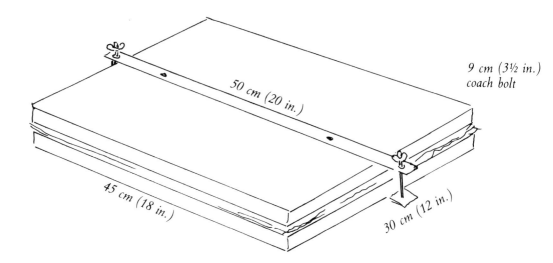

50 cm (20 in.)

45 cm (18 in.)

30 cm (12 in.)

9 cm (3½ in.)
coach bolt

41 The press will hold several layers of flowers at once.

lustre on the reverse side, whilst euonymus, an evergreen, has shiny leaves of a more enamelled appearance.

The colour of foliage is also important. In the autumn the colours will have turned from bronze to red through the shades to yellow. In the spring you will find the new young leaves, some even a deep shiny bronze, as with the *Clematis montana* turning later to a dull matt green, and the epimedium, which has pretty pink to red tinted leaves in spring. Grey leaves are to be found in abundance, and the reverse side in some is practically white. *Senecio greyii* has useful matt grey leaves oval in shape, and the underside is almost white. The silver poplar also has leaves which are white underneath and quite dark on their uppersides. This is a particularly beautiful member of the poplar family, as it blows in the

breeze the backs of the leaves shimmer in the sunlight. Even the humble blackberry, later in the year, has dark green to purple leaves on top whilst underneath they are light grey.

Variations in the shape of leaves must also be considered. Linear leaves are found in pinks, grasses and the pointed spikes of montbretia. Palmate leaves with deep lobes are found in the foliage of passion flowers and acers, and pinnate leaves on the jasmine plant. There are many other shapes which you will find in your search for material.

You will have gained some idea now of what kind of flowers, foliage and other material you should consider when preparing to make a picture. But always be on the lookout for any other specimens which might add something extra to your picture. Suggestions for other flowers and leaves to press will be found on page 80.

9
Preparing to press

Equipment

- Tweezers (eyebrow tweezers with flat ends)
- Small sharp scissors
- Secateurs
- Press (see page 48)
- Folded blotting paper to fit the press

NB Whichever type of press you use, whether it is a home-made press, a lightweight one, obtainable in different sizes from stationers or even toy shops, or whether a telephone directory or heavy book is used, the rules are the same.

Condition of flowers

It is no good going out into the garden after a shower and picking flowers protected as you hoped from the rain under a shrub or tree. They must be really dry, otherwise they will lose their colour and come out of the press a dull buff or brown.

The pollen is a vivid yellow in a fresh flower; and it will be brighter than some of its fellows who have been blooming for a day or so. Place your flowers face down or on their backs, whichever is the easier way. In some cases a little pressure with your thumb will ensure that they lie flat. Try and keep your material all of the same thickness. If very delicate blooms are put on the same sheet of paper as thicker ones, the fine ones will not receive the same amount of pressure as the more substantial specimens — also the coarser the flower, the longer it will take to dry. So keep your types of material separate.

When you come to use the contents of your press you may find that some of the petals fall off as you remove the specimen or that one or two stick to the paper. This is annoying, especially if it is a particularly good coloured or a well-shaped flower. A repair job can easily be done. Cut a small square of tissue or thin paper about 1 ¼ cm (½ in.) and place on it your chosen adhesive (one that dries transparent). Lie the damaged flower on this and with tweezers replace the missing petals. You may have to use another flower to do so, one perhaps where all the petals have not pressed very successfully. When well-stuck cut the paper away from the back using sharp, pointed scissors. This method can be used for repairing any type of flower, though if you have pressed enough the damaged blooms can be discarded.

10
Presses

A few years ago I visited a workshop that was making and selling commercially hundreds of pressed flower greetings cards. There in a converted farm shed several women were preparing material for pressing, by placing it between newspapers which were then put between railway sleepers; these were piled one on top of the other on shelves. Obviously there are many different ways of pressing, even telephone directories or heavy books will, with finer material, be quite satisfactory; but a really good pressed flower can only be obtained by hard pressing. Sometimes one opens an old book to find a spray of wild flowers beautifully pressed. It is easy to conjure up all sorts of romantic reasons for its presence there. Collecting and pressing flowers seems always to have been a very popular pastime.

Being very heavy, the railway sleepers did a good job resulting in well-pressed specimens, but railway sleepers would not be a good idea in your own home! I recommend a big heavy press, one that can easily be made at home by a handyman. For the best results flowers should be pressed between layers of blotting paper.

Materials for making a heavy press (fig. 41)

Measurements given for a press to take a standard piece of blotting paper, which when folded measures 44 cm x 29 cm (17½ in. x 11½ in.).
- Two pieces of chipboard or plywood, 1½ cm (½ in.) thick x 45 cm x 30 cm (18 in. x 12 in.).
- Two metal strips 50 cm x 2.5 cm (20 in. x 1 in.) and 3 mm (⅛ in.) thick with holes each end to take coach bolts, and two holes 7.5 cm (3 in.) from each end to enable screws to be inserted to hold the strips in place down the centre of each board.
- Four screws for attaching the strips to the boards.
- Two coach bolts 9 cm (3½ in.) with wing nuts.

The strips of metal are screwed one on the top board down the centre and the other under the centre of the bottom board. The coach bolts are inserted through the end holes so joining the two boards together. Cut two pieces of hardboard the size of the press to insert between the layers of blotting paper. This will enable you to press more than one layer of flowers.

A lightweight press

If you are going away on holiday and want to make a collection of flowers, take a lightweight press with you; these can be bought quite easily in various sizes. I have one which measures about 20 cm (8 in.) square. It has holes bored in each corner with bolts and wing nuts. Inside there are several layers of cardboard and blotting paper. Many wild flowers are protected species and it is an offence to pick them, so do find out which are 'forbidden fruit'. Conservation of flora is so important that this rule must be obeyed.

11
The process of pressing

If you want to press more than one layer of flowers, more padding will be needed, so place some sheets of newspaper between the blotting paper and the next layer of material. First fold a few sheets of newspaper to the size of the blotting paper, then arrange the flowers or leaves neatly in the blotting paper; cover with more sheets of newspaper and then place the first piece of hardboard in position. Repeat using the second piece of hardboard. The coach bolts are quite long enough to make a good sized 'sandwich'.

The length of time to leave the material in the press depends on the thickness of the specimens to be pressed. If you are in a hurry and you keep your press in the airing cupboard, the time for pressing can be about halved, but remember to turn the screws every day until you can no longer move them. It is not so easy to remember if the press is tucked away out of sight. Pressing for a week is long enough for delicate petalled flowers such as primulas and small violas; they should be paper-dry to the touch before use, if not screw down again and leave for a few more days. Heavier flowers such as roses need the longest time — about three to four weeks. After a week open up the press and with your tweezers carefully lift off the flower and, as the paper will be a little damp, move it to a dry spot. When placing these blooms on the blotting paper remember to leave room for moving. Repeat this once more about a week later, moving them back to the original spot. The drier the specimen becomes the more brittle it will be and the more liable to tear, so great care is needed.

Storing

When the material eventually comes out of the press the easiest way to store it is to leave it in the blotting paper in which it was pressed. Put it flat on a shelf in a dry cupboard or in a drawer. As the material accumulates you will have quite a pile of blotting paper. In order to save searching through sheets of paper to find a certain flower or leaf, label each sheet with a description of its contents (for example, foliage green, foliage brown) by sticking a piece of paper on the outside of the sheet to form a tab. It does save a lot of frustration and time when looking for a specific colour or specimen (*fig. 42a*).

Your blotting paper will last a long time and you will be able to use it over and over again.

42a Material stored and filed in blotting paper for easy reference.

12
Choosing the frames

At a recent exhibition of my pictures several people commented on my choice of frames and complimented me on the way they blended with the arrangement of flowers in the picture. If you have a particular colour scheme in mind, then you should look for a frame which will complement the arrangement but not dominate it. Alternatively, if you find one which you like and think suitable, then you must consider what colour flowers you will put in it. You can still find old frames by searching through antique or junk shops. Often you have to buy the frame complete with picture which will cost a little more. Many old frames will have suffered through the years and may if they are moulded gilt frames have lost a little of the moulding. Don't buy such a frame if a large amount has been broken off as it is too big a job to repair it efficiently, but if it is not in too bad a state it can be repaired fairly easily.

Simple repairs

Having pulled all the nails out and removed the backing, make sure that the frame is clean; brush out all the dust, and if there is the slightest sign of woodworm, paint over the surface with an anti-woodworm product (available from hardware shops). To repair damaged moulding use plastic padding (type elastic) which is also obtainable from hardware shops. This kind is slightly softer than the hard type and easier to rub down. Follow the instructions and, taking a small pointed knife, work the paste into shape, imitating the original moulding as nearly as you can. When it is dry use very fine sandpaper to rub the surface smooth. The repaired parts may then be painted with a good gold paint such as Treasure Gold. It may be necessary to paint the whole frame if you cannot match the gold well enough to conceal the repairs. A little raw umber from a tube of oil paint added to the gold paint will darken it if needed and make a better match with the original colour. The corners of an old frame may also have come a little apart. If they cannot be gently hammered back into place they can be filled in with plastic padding or plastic wood and the joins carefully painted to match.

Perhaps you would prefer not to be bothered with old frames, but I find them a challenge and I love discovering one and then deciding what to put in it. There are plenty of attractive modern frames obtainable from art shops and frame makers.

Mouldings

There is also a very wide choice of mouldings. You can get these made up or you can buy the mouldings by the metre and with the aid of a mitre block cut your angled corners and make your own frames. For a satisfactory result you will need clamps for the corners. There are various kinds on the market, and these will enable you to make a professional job of it.

When having frames made up, the following are useful sizes to consider: 25.5 cm x 20 cm (10 in. x 8 in.); 20 cm x 15 cm (8 in. x 6 in.); 15 cm x 10 cm (6 in. x 4 in.); and for a more elongated one used horizontally or upright, 33 cm x 23 cm (13 in. x 9 in.). These sizes have good proportions and I have used frames like these extensively.

Wooden oval frames are mostly imported from Italy, and are either of gold leaf or polished wood, sometimes with a gold leaf inner border. The sizes of these which I find most useful are 30 cm x 23 cm (12 in. x 9 in.), 25.5 cm x 18 cm (10 in. x 7 in.), and 18 cm x 13 cm (7 in. x 5 in.). These can also be obtained from art shops or frame-makers.

Be sure that the frames you buy are of good quality and made of wood so that tacks or veneer pins can be easily hammered into the backs. You cannot put nails into plastic or other compositions. It is possible to obtain mounts for most of the sizes quoted at costs upwards from £1. The addition of a mount to a narrow moulding often greatly improves a picture, besides leaving a smaller space to fill.

42b This picture and the one on p. 54 have been made as a pair. These two pressed flower arrangements in wooden frames with a gilt inner edge on a background of crimson taffeta evoke botanical pictures of an earlier age. The flowers, some of which have been pressed complete with their stems, are arranged somewhat stiffly, but full use has been made of the curving leaves which follow the shape of the frame, so bringing the whole design together. Flowers used in this picture include epimedium, Fritillaria meleagris, Primula auricula, Clematis macropetala and tulip.

42c This picture (a companion to fig. 42b) similarly has a shot-silk taffeta background of crimson. Again the leaves have been used to shape the arrangement. Material used includes a cream tulip on a straight stem, a curving stem of Fritillaria meleagris, *and lower down a bluebell spike.*

At the base is a silver leaf of Potentilla anserina, Alchemilla alpina *and* Tanacetum haradjanii, *finished with two auricular heads. To soften both designs clusters of gypsophila have been added.*

13
Fabric backgrounds

Background material as well as the frame must enhance and complement the group of flowers that forms the focal point of the picture. Apart from three-dimensional pictures (p. 68), for which I mostly use card, all the other pressed flower pictures are made on a background of silk or other fabric, mounted on cotton or polyester padding.

Pure silk, because of its subtle shades and the different textures according to type and quality, is the best to use but the most expensive. As you will be using so little the price you pay for a shade you like is well worth the extra cost. Pure silk is not too shiny as is sometimes the case with artificial silks, although these are quite acceptable if the weave is fine. Satin, if synthetic, must be of good quality, and it makes a very pretty background, but the cheaper satins have too shiny a surface. Shot silk or taffeta can be used effectively, and linens, cottons and felt for matt surfaces are all good materials which provide satisfactory backgrounds.

Colour in backgrounds

Often the choice of fabric will be influenced by the colour that you wish to use. Experience has shown that, generally speaking, the background colour must be fairly conservative. Shades of ivory to cream make the best background for groups of almost any colour flowers. Medium to dark shades of green will provide an effective background for yellows, whites and silvers, or use the contrast of a very dark brown or even black with white or silver leaves or flowers. A simple arrangement using field poppies and grasses on a soft yellow background produces a delightful picture. Figure 49 is an easily created picture of buttercups, grasses and daisies in a mount with a pale green background. Coral is another colour which, provided the flowers are bright enough to give a sufficient contrast, makes a pleasing group.

I have used deep red to very good effect with white flowers, but a picture of this colouring would not suit everybody's room or taste. I have not mentioned blue as a background, although on occasions I have used it, but it does not seem for some reason to be a good background colour. I find it preferable if I want a blue picture to use a very pale ivory, grey or just off-white background, and obtain the blues that I need in the flowers, so creating a blue picture on a pale background.

I have mentioned here a few of the colours I find most useful and of which I am most fond, but there are many other shades which you might care to try, and there is no reason why they should not make equally successful pictures.

If you have acquired a few pieces of fabric it is difficult to store them without finding that they have creased when you want to use them. Even folded in the packet in which you bought them and taken out as soon as you arrive home, they will sometimes have creases which in many fabrics are difficult to iron out. Materials are usually kept in the shop on cardboard rolls to prevent this happening and I have found that if you ask the shop assistants they will be glad to let you have an empty roll or two, no longer required by them. You can then keep your fabric on these and it will remain free from creases (*fig. 43*).

43 Keep fabric on rolls to prevent creasing.

14
Making the picture

Equipment

- Frame
- Hardboard cut to fit comfortably inside the frame
- Glass of similar size
- Padding — polyester or cotton as used for quilting
- Fabric for background
- UHU or similar clear adhesive
- Sharp scissors
- Fibre pen
- Tweezers

Backgrounds (fig. 44)

1 Place the hardboard on the padding.
2 Mark round the padding with the fibre pen close to the edges.
3 Cut round the padding.
4 Iron the fabric you are going to use.
5 Place the hardboard on the reverse side of the fabric. Cut round the fabric leaving 2½ cm (1 in.) on all sides.
6 Place the padding on the rough side of the hardboard. Cut it away if it overlaps.

7 Place fabric right side up on the padding with the grain of the material running straight up and down (i.e. parallel to the edge of the frame).
8 Carefully turn it over so that the fabric is underneath with the padding and the hardboard uppermost (a).
9 Cut across corners so that the fabric when stuck can be mitred at the corners if the picture is rectangular — if oval or circular, cut nicks all round the edges (b) (c) (d).
10 Run a line of adhesive round the edge of the hardboard about 1 cm (¼ in.) in and stick the material evenly all round, gently pulling it tight.

Backgrounds with mounts

1 Measure the opening in the mount.
2 Cut the padding 2½ cm (1 in.) bigger all round than the aperture.
3 Place the padding on the rough side of the hardboard using a dab of adhesive to fix it.
4 Cut the fabric 2½ cm (1 in.) bigger than the hardboard all round, and finish as previously explained.

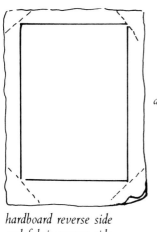

a

hardboard reverse side
and fabric wrong side

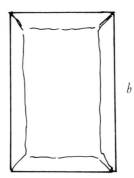

b

fabric mitred at
corners and stock on
back of hardboard

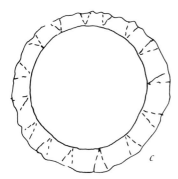

c

circular frame
with nicks cut out

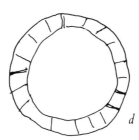

d

fabric stuck
smoothly onto
back of hardboard

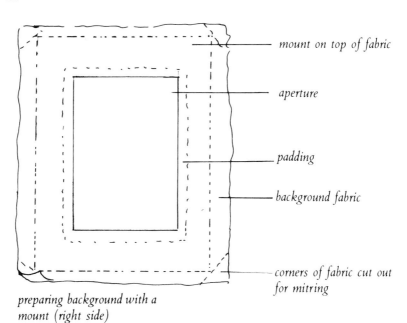

— mount on top of fabric

— aperture

— padding

— background fabric

— corners of fabric cut out
for mitring

preparing background with a
mount (right side)

44 Backgrounds for mounts.

15
Choosing the material

Search through your stock of pressed flowers, and with your tweezers pick out the material you think you will need to make your picture. If you have put labelled tabs on your blotting paper your search will be comparatively easy as you will know where to find the specimens you require. Place all the material on a piece of white card or blotting paper, making it easier to see the colours and shapes.

16
Using the free method

In my previous books, two methods of making pictures were described: the free method and the fixed method. The free method uses no adhesive to fix the flowers, relying solely on the pressure of the glass and the padding to hold the material firmly in place. The other way is to stick all the material on the background using a thinner padding or even card. For the purposes of this book I use the free method for all the pictures which have a padded backing. By adopting this method you can arrange your material, rest the glass on it, look at it again, remove the glass and make any alterations that may be necessary before finally nailing the glass in. There is no reason though, once you know exactly where your material is to be placed, why you shouldn't stick some of the background pieces, such as the outline which will make your shape. So, until you are really experienced and able to nail your glass in without disturbing the arrangement, you could stick some of the material and leave the rest.

Pick up with your tweezers the pieces that will make the outline of your picture. With the frame in place, starting at the top and then the bottom, first form the outline of the shape you want the arrangement to take. Work from the outside to the centre, using the biggest flowers to make the focal point. This can be in the centre of the picture or lower down according to the design decided upon.

Although one doesn't want a totally symmetrical picture, it must balance and, depending upon design, some of the material must be equidistant from the sides of the frame. If you intend to stick some of the material, use an adhesive which will dry clear, such as Bostic 'Stick 'n fix'. Squeeze a drop onto a small saucer or jam-pot lid, and taking a pin or darning needle, put the smallest dab on the back of the material. This will be enough to fix it.

17
Finishing the picture

Equipment

- A small hammer
- 13 mm veneer pins
- 15 mm veneer pins
- A clean soft cloth
- Masking tape
- Adhesive (Stick 'n fix, Glu stick or Copydex)
- Pliers
- Scissors
- A small paint brush
- Coloured paper or good quality wallpaper for backing
- Screw-eyes
- Picture wire

Method

1 Making sure your hands are clean, wash the glass and dry well using the soft cloth. Be careful when handling the cleaned glass to leave no finger marks.
2 Using the paint brush, work over the background of the picture, removing all specks and dust.

3 Place the glass over the picture and lay on the frame. Holding the glass and frame firmly in place turn the picture onto its face.
4 Hammer in two or three pins — enough to fix the frame in position.
5 Turn the picture face up again and look carefully to make sure nothing has jumped out of place or a hidden speck has been dislodged.
6 If all is well turn over again and hammer in the veneer pins at about 5 cm (2 in.) intervals. Hammer the pins as flat as possible against the sides of the frame. If the frame is a shallow one the nails may need a padding of masking tape before the backing paper is finally put on.
7 Mark with a pencil on the backing paper the outline of the frame and cut out.
8 Rub the adhesive onto the frame and round the edge of the backing paper and stick it onto the back of the picture. I use my fingers to do this.
9 Insert the screw-eyes and attach the picture wire.

18
Designs for pictures

In the following pages you will find designs for different types of pressed flower pictures with step by step instructions for their creation.

Design 1: Leaves, grasses and seedheads (fig. 45)

This picture, shown in fig. 46, is in an oval frame and consists of various leaves of different colours and textures including some sprays of grass, silver discs of honesty, seed capsules and some petals of skeletonized hydrangea flowers.

46 The completed picture

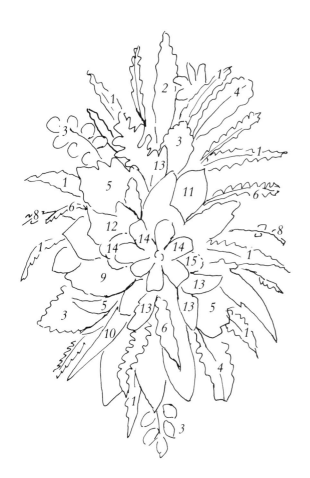

45 Design 1. Leaves and grasses.

The order in which the material is arranged (and number of each required): 1 bracken leaflets (8); 2 and 6 grasses (4); 3 rose leaves (4); 4 Tanacetum hardajanii (2); 5 Clematis montana (3); 7 cineraria (1); 8 thyme (8); 9 euonymus (1); 10 willow (1); 11 honesty discs (2); 12 ivy (2); 13 leaflets of silverweed (5); 14 Alchemilla alpina (2); 15 skeletonized hydrangea petals (2).

*1 A Victorian-style picture in a gilt frame. Numerous flowers
have been used in the creation of this arrangement.*

2 **(Top)** *Passion flowers are ideal for paper collage with their distinctive shape and curling tendrils.*
(Right) *Paeonia clusii—made in paper collage from a book of botanical paintings and prints.*
(Left) *This collage was adapted from an old Chinese painting on silk.*

3 *The small group upper left measures 10 cm (4 in.). The honey-coloured silk background blends well with the deeper colour of the maplewood frame and the flowers which tone with it. White and silver flowers 'grow' out of the rectangular frame on the left. The small wooden oval frame encloses a group of claret-coloured flowers on a yellow silk background.*

he arrangement is in a brown wooden oval
ame with a gold inner edge. The background is
f cream satin, and the frame measures 28 cm x 23
m (11 in. x 9 in.). The group itself measures 18
m x 11 cm (7 in. x 4½ in.). First the outline is
efined by eight leaflets of bracken with a spray
f grass at the top and a small spray of yellow rose
aves at the base. The outline is further
rengthened by the addition of leaves of roses,
leagnus, *Clematis montana*, cineraria and *Tanacetum
uradjanii*. Towards the centre are two honesty
iscs, leaves of ivy and silverweed, while the
entre itself is covered by ivy and two leaves of
lchemilla alpina with petals of skeletonized
ydrangea flowers added. Grasses are finally
icluded to soften the outline (*fig . 45*).

The colours of the material range from silver
white to grey and from pale straw yellow
through red to the deep bronze of the montana.
Dark green is supplied by the ivy leaves.

Design 2: A Victorian picture

Any group of flowers in an antique frame evokes
a Victorian atmosphere, especially if it has quite a
quantity of material in it, all arranged closely
together (*fig. 47*). The same effect can be obtained
also by using modern gilt frames. Old maple
wood frames are very difficult to come by now-
a-days, although big ones are sometimes to be
found. These would have to be cut down to the

47 *Design 2. A Victorian group.*

The order in which the material is arranged. **1**
Willow leaf; **2** *Stem of Leucojum;* **3** *Lady's
bedstraw;* **4** *silverweed (2);* **5** *rose leaf;* **6** *leaf of cow
parsley;* **7** *stem of bluebells;* **8** *spray of hydrangea
flowers;* **9** *clematis leaf;* **10** *silver willow leaf;* **11**
mauve primula; **12** *cluster of anaphlis;* **13** *leaf of
Alchemilla alpina;* **14** *red tulip;* **15** *dark purple
primula;* **16** *canary bird rose;* **17** *crimson potentilla;*
18 *purple primula;* **19** *passion flower;* **20**
mauve/yellow pansy; **21** *Anemone blanda;* **22**
feverfew (2); **23** *white xeranthemum;* **24** *gentian;*
25 *apricot primula;* **26** *daisy;* **27** *primrose;* **28**
bluebell flower; **29** *feverfew;* **30** *heather;* **31** *head of
cow parsley. The flowers numbered 23-31 can be
slipped under the material already in place. Other
leaves used include more silver willow, silverweed,
clematis, rose and ivy.*

required size, needing the skill of a handyman to mitre the corners successfully.

Art shops sell modern maple frames which for lack of the antique variety I find quite satisfactory. They make delightful pictures, using a background to tone with the warm shades of the veneer, adding soft coloured flowers to complement the whole. With the harder colour of a gold frame, brighter and more brilliant combinations can be introduced.

This picture is Victorian in style. It is in an oval gold leaf frame measuring 39 cm x 30 cm (15 in. x 12 in.). The background is a very pale green slub silk. In the picture there are 18 different kinds of flowers and 10 different leaves. It is the variety of the material which gives interest to a massed arrangement of flowers.

If you have not got some of the flowers in the picture it should not be difficult to substitut different ones, at the same time maintaining th basic shapes and sizes of the flowers. The colou of the arrangement can be left to your artisti sense.

Block in the outline of the picture first, startin at the top with a willow leaf and a spray c leucojum. At the bottom place the lady bedstraw, a leaf of silver weed, a dark rose lea and a small leaf of cow parsley. These will giv you the width of the arrangement. Strengthen th outline with a stem of bluebells, a spray of sma hydrangea flowers, a *Clematis montana* leaf and silver willow leaf.

Figure 47 shows the order in which to place th main material. Extra flowers or leaves can b added where necessary to complete the pictur and fill in any gaps.

19
Pictures in the Dutch style

Dutch flower pieces, which date from the sixteenth century, owed their popularity to the growing interest in horticulture. Flemish refugee painters were the first to produce these paintings. Mixed flowers of vivid, sometimes garish, colours were arranged in vases and painted against a dark background. The flowers were not necessarily in proportion to the container, indeed in some pictures they appear to be top heavy. The blossoming times of the flowers seem also to have been disregarded, the blooms of spring, summer and autumn being mixed as the artist chose. Some bouquets were flooded with a hard, even light, while in other paintings the light falls from one or other side gradating into a deep shadow towards the back. The flowers in many cases are very stiff

and formal whilst others have a beautifu flamboyance.

I have tried to imitate some of the principles c the Dutch flower paintings using big flowers hig up in the arrangement with the light falling dow the centre by choosing pale-coloured flowers an foliage and with the shadow defined by dar material on either side. In other pictures the ligh falls from right or left. Reproductions of Dutc paintings are easily found on greetings cards o postcards. Study these before you start making picture. I have several books of reproduction which I always refer to when embarking o another picture. A wonderful collection of Dutc flower paintings is to be found at the Fitzwillia Museum in Cambridge bequeathed by Majo

Henry Broughton, who later became the second Lord Fairhaven. For lovers of flowers and flower paintings, a visit to the Museum is a most rewarding experience. When exhibiting some of my pressed flower pictures in London recently I included a 'Dutch' one in a large antique frame. My pleasure was intense on hearing someone amongst several people around my stand say to his companion 'This picture looks exactly like a seventeenth-century Dutch painting'. I was delighted to be able to say to him that it was exactly what the picture was intended to represent.

Dutch pictures are big, so you will need a frame approximately 58 cm x 45 cm (23 in. x 17 in.) — anything bigger would be too difficult to work with. An oak frame with a gold inset to lighten it is very suitable and would cost around £5, unless it is being sold for the picture in it. The frame will cost considerably more if you have it made at an art shop, but you will have a wide choice of mouldings. You will need a piece of hardboard and glass to fit the frame. Use a polyester padding which is a little more 'bouncy' than cotton and will hold the material more firmly. Select a dark-coloured fabric for the background, with a slight shine. Stick it tightly on the back so that the padding feels firm to the touch.

Most Dutch pictures have bowls or vases in which the flowers are arranged. These can be made of leaves or even petals if of a suitable colour and size. All you have to create is the suggestion that a vase is there with flowers arranged in it, (fig. 48). It is a good idea with vases in mind to have a collection of fairly big, different coloured leaves.

Decide on the shape of your vase, draw it on a piece of paper and cut it out. Then stick the leaves on the paper to form the vase. If you haven't suitably shaped leaves you may have to cut them to the correct shape. The size of the vase will depend on the size of the frame you are using. This is where your artistic eye comes in. I find the vase is usually a little smaller than it would be in real life.

Once you have decided where the vase is to be, stick it in place complete with paper backing. In the paintings the arrangement is usually standing on a marble slab or table. Indicate this by using a

crayon suitable for use on fabrics such as Pentel Dye Sticks.

Now you can search for your material. Lay it on the background as you find it, roughly where you think it should go. If you have some reproductions of Dutch paintings as a guide, you will have a good idea what you need, although it goes without saying that there is no way a Dutch masterpiece can be reproduced exactly, flower for flower. The fall of the light and the recession into shadow, however, can be imitated, and if you have a collection of colourful flowers you can also copy the shapes and approximate size of the blooms in the picture.

I think flowers are too beautiful to make them look like something they are not; although butterflies can be made out of petals, to do so does not appeal to me nor do I care to use squashed ladybirds or beetles, so sadly my Dutch pictures must do without any insect life. But I am not averse to putting in a leaf with a hole in it, or to the use of flowers or leaves to create a vase. On one occasion I was lucky enough to acquire some bee orchids. I had no hesitation in using these poised strategically over the arrangement. That kitchen garden pest, the cabbage butterfly, could be used if you really want to, but as I haven't done so, I must leave it to you to work out the killing and pressing processes!

Snakes head fritillaries appear in many Dutch flower pieces. I include these when I can. In the wild they are a protected species and are rare and of course picking them is forbidden. I grow them specially to include in my pictures. Tulips are very frequently used, particularly the striped and parrot varieties, as well as different coloured auriculas, roses and carnations (difficult to use pressed), convolvulus, iris, narcissus and paeonies. Any flower that we can grow will be found in Dutch paintings.

It is a most interesting challenge to try to copy with pressed flowers some of the superb master-pieces of the sixteenth and seventeenth centuries.

Design 3: A Dutch flower piece

The Dutch-style picture illustrated in colour plate 4 is in a frame, the measurements of which are 58 cm x 43 cm (23 in. x 17 in.). The group of

48 Design 3. A Dutch flower piece.

Order of arranging flowers. **1** *lavender spike;* **2** *leucojum;* **3** *pink tulips (2);* **4** *deeper pink tulip;* **5** *open red tulip;* **6** *fritillary;* **7** *achillea leaves (2);* **8** *viola;* **9** Anthemis tinctoria; **10** *Passion flowers (2);* **11** *white xeranthemum;* **12** *lily. Other flowers include bird cherry, anaphalis, hydrangea, forget-me-not, cow parsley,* Alchemilla mollis, Cineraria cruenla *(the pot plant), cowslip, auricula, feverfew, common daisy. Other leaves include: silver poplar, Alchemilla alpina, acer, ivy, cow parsley.*

flowers measures 43 cm x 30 cm (17 in. x 12 in.). This is really the maximum size that you can safely make to ensure that the material will remain in place by the pressure of the glass. Polyester padding which has more bounce is used, and the fabric is a very dark green taffeta. The table on which the vase stands is indicated by drawing the outline with a Pentel stick and lightly shading in. At least 24 different kinds of flowers have been used to make this picture and eight kinds of leaves. You almost certainly would be unable to copy this picture flower for flower, but substitutes can be used with as good effect.

The daisy shapes of anthemis and xeranthemum can be replaced with single chrysanthemums or ox-eye daisies. Single roses could replace the passion flowers, and for lilies use alstroemeria. These can in season be obtained from the florist, if you do not grow them yourself. Field poppies could be used for the flowers that appear to be in shadow. On the dark background they will be nearly invisible, so giving depth to the arrangement.

The container is made first. This consists of eleven silver willow leaves, nine for the vase itself and two for the base. In this picture the light falls from the left, so place more pale material on that side.

Make the outline or shape of the arrangement first, starting at the top with lavender, leucojum, montbretia, two large pale pink tulips on the left, a deeper coloured one lower down on the right and an open one just above the vase on the left. Place the fritillary low down on the right to balance the arrangement, which because of its dark colour will indicate the shade on that side of the picture.

Add the two leaves of achillea and then fill the centre in, starting high up with a pansy, anthemis, passion flowers, bird cherry, lilies, garden daisies and auriculas. The order in which to arrange the main flowers is shown in the numbered diagram (*fig. 48*). As you continue, fill in with the smaller leaves sprays and flowers. Remember to see that flowers and leaves fall over the edge of the vase.

Finally, place some leaves and a flower on the surface of the 'table'. In this picture there are a violet and forget-me-not and a leaf of cow parsley.

20
Flowers in mounts

A mount can greatly improve your picture. Also a much narrower moulding can be used, and with a mount added a cheap frame can be made to look quite important. Your flowers can 'grow' out of the base of your mount or they can be arranged conventionally in the centre of the picture. Flowers such as passion flowers used alone produce a most effective arrangement, as do roses, poppies and many others. A quantity of very small flowers used in a dense group is another pleasing way to make a picture in a mount. You will need a lot of practice if you use tiny flowers and will have to be very dexterous with your tweezers — but to help the arrangement stay in place you can always resort to using a little adhesive.

Design 4: Spring flowers in a meadow (fig. 49)

In this picture (*fig. 49*) the flowers and leaves 'grow' from the base of the arrangement. It has a pale green cotton satin background and is surrounded by a dark green mount set in a dull gold frame. The overall measurement of the picture is 32.5 cm x 28 cm (13 in. x 11 in.), and the inside of the mount measures 20 cm x 15 cm (8 in. x 6 in.). Flowers from the fields have been used, six buttercups with long curving stems, all but two of them in profile, four buttercup buds and nine common daisies with four in profile showing deep pink tips on the reverse of the petals. Spikes of grass complete the arrangement with one spray of bluebell buds added to balance the daisies on the opposite side.

49 Design 4. Spring flowers in a meadow.

50 *Design 4 comprises buttercups in flower and bud,*
daisies, grass and a bluebell.

21
Pictures using three dimensions

Pictures using three dimensions offer a new challenge. The flowers, instead of looking what they are, flat and pressed, appear to be alive but imprisoned behind glass. A background of coloured card is cut to fit into the frame which must be deep enough to take a hardboard backing, the card background, one layer of perspex and one of glass (two layers of perspex if the picture is to have even more depth). Perspex is used for the inner layers of the picture rather than glass as two or three layers of glass would make the whole rather heavy. I use glass for the top layer, as perspex is very vulnerable to scratches — even a gentle rub with a soft cloth can mark the surface. Perspex is quite easily obtainable. Your DIY shop will order it for you cut to size or, you can find the names of suppliers from whom you can buy direct under plastics in a commercial telephone directory.

First, collect the material from your store and lay all the flowers and leaves on the background to make a complete picture. Having done this, with everything arranged to your satisfaction, at this stage you may say, 'why bother, the picture looks nice as it is', in which case forget dimensional pictures and read no further! If, however, you wish to go on you must decide which of the material should remain in the background and which should come forward onto the next layer. Using, always, the minimum of adhesive, stick the flowers you are sure about on the card background and then place the perspex on top. Be very careful doing this as perspex has more static electricity than glass and if your flowers are not firmly stuck down they may fly up onto the underside of the perspex. Having covered the base, you then arrange the remaining material on the perspex. This must also be carefully stuck, allowing none of the adhesive to show round the edges. This will not occur if only a small drop is used. The outer layer of glass is finally put in place and your picture is complete, apart of course from your finishing the picture (see p. 59).

(see p. 59).

Here follow four designs, the last three of which (6, 7 and 8) are all made in the same size and coloured frames. The rebate is 1 cm (½ in.) deep, which is enough to hold two or three layers of perspex or glass and the card or board for the background. The frames measure 32.5 cm x 25.5 cm (13 in. x 10 in.) and are of dulled mottled silver.

Design 5: Late winter (fig. 51 and 52)

Figure 51 shows a simple three-dimensional picture on two layers. This consists of eight

51 Design 5. Late winter. This picture is made in two layers to give a three-dimensional effect.

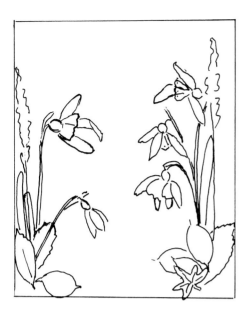

52 *Step 1. Material arranged and stuck on the black card background.*
Step 2. Material forming the top layer stuck onto perspex.

snowdrops, some fully out, some buds — it is important not to have all the same flowers looking exactly alike. You will also need seven snowdrop leaves; three heads of grass seed; four honesty flowers; three leaves of variegated euonymus; three ivy leaves; and two skeletonized hydrangea flowers. The small rectangular picture [20 cm x 15 cm (8 in. x 6 in.)] has a black card background. The flowers 'grow' from the base. Two spikes of grass are placed on either side with two snowdrop leaves and there are two snowdrops on the left and three on the right. The base of the stems is concealed by euonymus leaves and honesty and one ivy leaf (*fig 52a*). The final layer has the remaining snowdrops, one on the left and two on the right, placed so that the snowdrops behind are easily visible, and more leaves and honesty finish the arrangement with two skeletonized hydrangea flowers set low down (*fig. 52b*).

Design 6: 'White and silver' (fig. 53)

A three-layered picture which will give greater depth goes a step further in the search for something different. The method is exactly the same, except that you have three layers of flowers: on the black card background, in the middle between two layers of perspex, and the third layer on the top piece of perspex covered by the piece of glass. This type of picture needs more planning as you have to take care to arrange the material in such a way that a flower on the bottom layer is not hidden entirely by material on the two subsequent layers, otherwise there would be no reason to have a flower there at all. Figures show the placing of the material layer by layer. On the bottom layer are two *Clematis montana*, one in profile, a spray of bird cherry, a hydrangea flower, sprays of gypsophila and three leaves of silverweed. The middle layer has two *Clematis montana* flowers, a head of candytuft, one xeranthemum flower, silverweed, a spike of grass, a vine leaf, a silver poplar leaf, one leaf of alpine alchemilla reversed to show the satin underside, a head of cow parsley and a skeleton leaf. The final or top layer consists of a leaf of alpine alchemilla reversed, a spray of gypsophila, one hydrangea flower, a spike of grass, one skeletonized lavatera seed head and a clematis seed head. This may sound a very complicated process with such a large amount of material

*53 Design 6. A pressed flower picture made in three tiers.
The xeranthemums on the upper layer catch the light and
appear to be standing well forward.*

apparently used, but if you add up the number of different types of flowers and leaves actually required you will find that there are no more than 6.

54 Design 6. White and silver: (a), (b), and (c) show how the three layers are built up; (d) shows the finished arrangement.

(a) **1** *bird cherry;* **2** Clematis montana; **3** *honesty seed head;* **4** *silverweed (3);* **5** *gypsophila (2);* **6** *hydrangea.*

(b) **1** *bird cherry;* **2** *silverweed;* **3** Clematis montana; **4** *spray of grass;* **5** *Hare's tail grass;* **6** Alchemilla alpina; **7** *leaf of silver poplar;* **8** *vine leaf;* **9** *skeletonized leaf;* **10** *head of candytuft;* **11** *xeranthemum (2);* **12** *cow parsley.*

(c) **1** *xerantheum (2);* **2** *leaves of* Alchemilla alpina *(2);* **3** *spray of grass;* **4** *gypsophila;* **5** *skeletonized flowers of hydrangea;* **6** *clematis seed head;* **7** *anaphalis.*

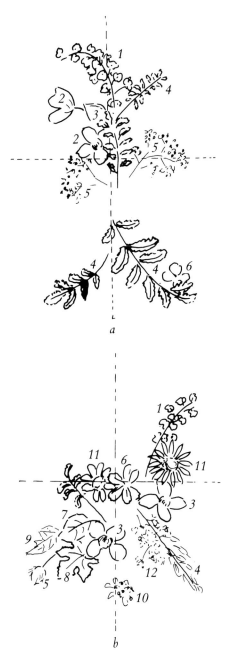

Design 7: A bunch of flowers (fig. 57)

The picture in fig. 57 is in the form of a bunch of flowers and is made in two layers. It is a picture requiring fairly substantial material. Made on white board, the bottom layer has a red poppy, a cream tulip, one yellow alstroemeria flower, one canary bird rose, one white xeranthemum flower, two poppy seed heads and one bud, two sprays of quaking grass, one spray of *Statice suworowii* and two stems to form part of the stalks which make the bunch. The top layer consists of a montbretia spray, a purple viola, a yellow anthemis flower, two xeranthemum flowers, a canary bird rose and a small cream tulip. Leaves of ivy, rose, silverweed, alpine alchemilla, silver willow, silver poplar and artemesia are added with two blades of grass for a spiky effect and a stem of quaking grass, and finally six stems of varying thickness and length, the tops concealed under the poplar leaf.

57 *The completed picture.*

b

a

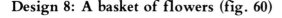

58 Design 7. (a) lower layer; (b) upper layer.

Design 8: A basket of flowers (fig. 60)

Figures 58 (a) and (b) show the building up of this design on a buff background arranged in two layers. The lower layer is made up of a stem of toadflax, hare's tail grass, cow parsley, artemesia, fern, polygonum and a cluster of privet buds (which becomes brown when pressed). The upper layer is dominated by two large single xeranthemums and a yellow anthemis flower. The white satin sheen of the xeranthemums is echoed by the two silvery leaves of silver weed and willow close by and a nearly open bud of xeranthemum higher up in the arrangement. The centre is supported by some bright yellow wallflowers and two buttercups. A cluster of anaphalis flowers balances the leaf on the left, while clematis flowers, a viola, forget-me-nots and a daisy radiate outwards. The 'basket' is made up of ten straw-coloured leaflets of bracken stuck onto the upper layer of the arrangement.

59 The finished arrangement with the two layers in place.

74

60 Design 8. Two layers of pressed flowers make this picture. The basket is placed on the upper layer with most of the bigger flowers.

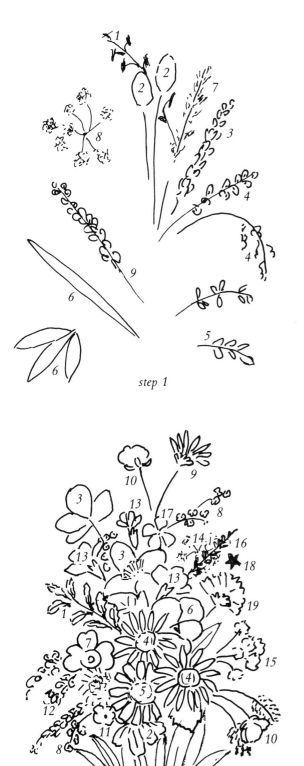

step 1

step 2

completed picture

61 Design 8. A basket of flowers.

62 *Alpine flowers collected on an Austrian holiday. The flowers include snowbells, gentians, oxlips, marsh marigolds, yellow wood violets, and an alpine buttercup.*

22
Glossary of floral characteristics

This list includes some flowers and leaves which are all useful and can be pressed. I have also added some wild flowers. Remember that the ancestors of the flowers we cultivate in our gardens once grew in the wild in many parts of the world. Specimens have been collected by botanists over the centuries and brought back to this country where they have flourished and become today what we recognise as our garden flowers. The weeds which we pull up in the garden we call wild flowers when we find them growing in fields, woods or hedgerows.

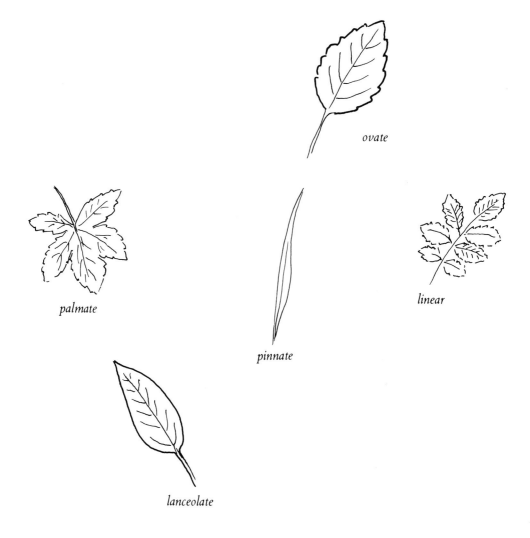

ovate

palmate

pinnate

linear

lanceolate

63 Leaf shapes.

Botanical terms

Annual	A plant which completes its life cycle in one year
Anther	Part of the stamen holding the pollen.
Biennial	A plant which requires two years to complete its life cycle
Calyx	Part of the flower which holds the petals
Corolla	Petals partially or wholly fused together
Corona	The crown of the flower (i.e. the trumpet of a daffodil)
Deciduous	A plant shrub or tree which loses its leaves in the autumn
Evergreen	A plant shrub or tree bearing foliage throughout the year
Floret	A small individual flower forming part of a large head or cluster (i.e. a daisy)
Lanceolate	Leaves which are narrow and tapering at each end
Linear	Leaves which are long, narrow and pointed
Ovate	Leaves which are oval or egg-shaped
Palmate	Leaves which are hand-shaped and divided into more than three leaflets arising from a central point
Perennial	A plant which lives indefinitely
Pinnate	Leaves arranged on opposite sides of a common stalk
Pistil	Female organ of the flower
Raceme	Flowers growing from one central stem (i.e. a cowslip)
Sepal	A leaf of the calyx
Stamen	The male reproductive organ of a plant surmounted by the anther containing pollen grains

The following lists of flowers have been divided into flower shapes or formations — with columns giving the common name, variety, colour and notes. Where a specimen is described as transparent, it should either be mounted on similar coloured tissue paper, or one flower should be placed on top of another.

Abbreviations

A	Annual
B	Biennial
Bb	Bulb
Cl	Climber
C	Corm
D	Deciduous
E	Evergreen
P	Perennial
Sh	Shrub
T	Tree
Tb	Tuber
W	Wild

64 Parts of a flower.

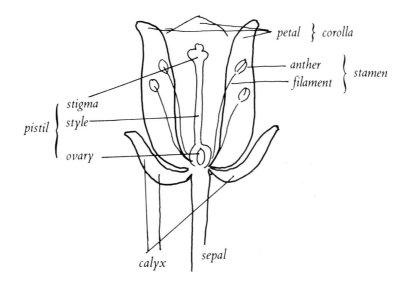

79

Flower shapes

I Single (four five or six petals)

Name	Variety		Colour	Notes
Anemone	*Tb*	*A. blanda*	white, pink, blue	
		A. coronaria (St Brigid)	strong colours	
		A. fulgens	vermillion	
		A. hybrida (Japanese anemone)	pink, white	centres useful for using with other flowers
Anemone	*W*	*A. nemorosa*	white	the wood anemone
Buttercup	*W*	*Ranunculus acris*	yellow	flowers and buds
Clematis	*Cl*	*C. montana alba*	white	⎰young leaves turn
		C. montana rubens	pink	⎱nearly black with satin sheen
Hellebore	*P*	*Helleborus foetidus*	green	
		H. niger (Christmas rose)	white	flowers and leaves
		H. orientalis (Lenten lily)	mauve, purple,	
		H. viridis	green	
Cranesbill	*P*	*Geranium ibericum*	violet blue	⎰leaves turn dark
		G. psilostemon	deep magenta	⎱orange red
Heartsease	*W*	*Viola tricolor*	yellow, purple, white	excellent for small arrangements
Jasmine	*Sh*	*Jasminum nudiflorum*	yellow	single star-shaped flowers
		J. officinale	white	leaf sprays and flowers
Pansy	*P*	*Viola* many varieties		bi-colour best
Passion flower	*Cl*	*Passiflora caerulea*	green, blue	pistil and stamens separately tendrils and leaves
Poached egg flower	*A*	*Limnanthes douglasii*	yellow edged, white,	transparent
Poppy	*W*	*Papaver rhoeas* (field poppy)	bright red	mount on red tissue paper to strengthen colour
Potentilla	*P*	*P. atrosanguinea*	scarlet	leaves and flowers
Potentilla	*Sh*	*P. fruticosa*	apricot, cream, red, white	
Primrose	*W*	*Primula vulgaris*	pale yellow	some flowers transparent, press buds
Rose	*Sh*	*Rosa* 'American Pillar'	pink	⎰all single roses
	Cl	*R.* 'Canary Bird'	yellow	⎱press
		R. 'Wedding Day'	cream	well
Rose	*W*	*Rosa canina*	pink, white	
St John's Wort	*Sh*	*Hypericum olympicum*	yellow	
Tobacco plant	*A*	*Nicotiana affinis*	green, white	
Violet	*W*	*Viola riviniana*	blue, violet	profile also
Wallflower	*P*	*Cheiranthus cheiri*	cream, orange, red, yellow	

II Daisy-shaped flowers

Name		Variety	Colour	Notes
Anthemis	P	A. cupaniana	white yellow centre	
		A. tinctoria	lemon yellow centre	
Chrysanthemum	A	C. caranatum	orange, red, yellow, with rings of other colours	
Cineraria	Sh	C. cruenta	blue, mauve pink, white	grown as pot plants, bi-coloured most effective
Daisy	W	Bellis perennis (common daisy)	white sometimes tinged with pink	flowers buds and reverse
Doronicum	P	D. cordatum	yellow	early spring transparent
Feverfew	W	Tanacetum parthenium	white, yellow centre	
Marigold	A	Calendula officinalis	yellow, orange	transparent
Xeranthemum	A	X. annum	lilac, pink, white	flowers have attractive satin sheen

III Multi-headed or clusters

Name		Variety	Colour	Notes
Achillea	P	A. filipendulina	yellow	flat heads press pieces
Agapanthus (African lily)	P	'Headbourne Hybrids'	dark blue pale blue	bell-shaped flowers — use singly and for vases
Allium	Bb	A. moly	yellow	terminal umbels
		A. ostrowskianum	pink	also use single flowers
Alstroemeria	P	A. aurantiaca	yellow, pink, cream, orange	trumpet-shaped use single flower and buds
Anaphalis (Pearl everlasting)	P	A. triplinervis	pearly white	clusters and single flowers
Astrantia	P	A. major	green or pink	
Ceanothus	Sh	many varieties	blue	tiny flowers in bunches; press whole
Chionodoxa (Glory of the snow)	Bb	C. luciliae	blue or white eye	several flowers on loose racemes; press whole and single flowers
Choisya	Sh	C. ternata	white	use single flowers
Cow parsley	W	Anthriscus sylvestris	white	many varieties of the umbelliferae family all press well
Cowslip	W	Primula veris	yellow	flowers on loose racemes; press whole and single
Elder	T	Sambucus canadensis	buds green, flowers cream	press clusters of buds at all stages clusters of flowers
Guelder rose	Sh	Viburnum opulus	cream white	press single flowers and small clusters

Name	Variety		Colour	Notes
Hydrangea	*Sh*	*H. macrophylla*	blue, pink, white	use single flowers
		H. petiolaris	white	
Lilac	*Sh*	*Syringa* many varieties	shades of lilac also white	press small clusters fade to light brown
Narcissus	*Bb*	small varieties, e.g. Soleil d'Or	yellow white	press single flowers; nick trumpet to flatten
Ornithogalum	*Bb*	*O. umbellatum* (Star of Bethlehem)	white, green stripe	transparent
Phlox	*A*	*P. drummondii*	pinks, purple, red, white	use single flowers
Privet	*Sh*	*Ligustrum ovalifolium*	cream	flowers borne on panicles; press whole
Verbena	*A*	various	purple, crimson, pink, red	press whole; terminal clusters; single flowers
Viburnum	*Sh*	*V. carlesii*	white	use single flowers
		V. tinus (laurustinus)	white or pink tinted	press whole heads
Yarrow	*W*	*Achillea millefolium*	white, sometimes pink	

IV Spikes and Sprays

Name	Variety		Colour	Notes
Alchemilla	*P*	*A. mollis*	lime green	minute flowers; press small sprays
Bird cherry	*T*	*Prunus padus*	white	sprays
Bluebell (Wild hyacinth)	*W*	*Endymion nonscriptus*	blue	sprays with terminal flowers in bud
Catmint	*P*	*Nepeta x faassenii*	blue mauve	spikes
Deutzia	*Sh*	varieties	white, pink, purple	
Forget-me-not	*P*	*Myosotis alpestris*	blue, royal,	sprays
		M. sylvatica	blue, pink	
Fuchsia	*Sh*	*F. magellanica* and varieties	crimson, purple	press single flowers; small sprays
Gypsophila	*P*	*G. elegans*	white, pink	small sprays
		G. paniculata	white	
Grape hyacinth	*Bb*	*Muscari* various	blue, white	press whole and seed heads later
Heather	*P*	*Erica* various	pink, white	
Heuchera	*P*	*H. sanguinea*	pink	sprays
Larkspur	*HA*	*Delphinium ajacis*	pink, blue, white	sprays, single flowers, buds
Lavender	*Sh*	*Lavendula spica*	lilac	
Lily of the Valley	*P*	*Convallaria majalis*	white, pink	press whole; turns cream
London Pride	*P*	*Saxifraga umbrosa*	pink	sprays
Montbretia	*Bb*	*Crocosmia x crocosmiiflora*	orange	single flowers; buds in sprays
Russian vine	*Cl*	*Polygonum baldschuanicum*	white	sprays

Name	Variety		Colour	Notes
Scilla	Bb	S. bifolia	blue	sprays, single flowers
Tiarella	P	T. cordifolia (foam flower)	cream	sprays, leaves
Veratrum	P	V. nigrum	very dark	small star-like flowers; black when pressed

V Bell- or funnel-shaped

Name	Variety		Colour	Notes
Freesia	C	varieties	red, yellow, orange, mauve, pink, white	single and sprays
Fritillary	Bb	Fritillaria meleagris (snake's head)	cream, purple, chequered	protected in the wild
Gentian	P	Gentiana varieties	deep blue	keeps colour well
Godetia	A	G. amoena	lilac, crimson, white	press in profile; petals have satin sheen
Lily	Bb	Lilium martagon	mauve, white	} small lilies preferable
		L. pyrenaicum and varieties	orange, yellow	
Snowdrop	Bb	Galanthus nivalis	green, white	double single
Snowflake	Bb	Leucojum vernum	green, white	single and sprays
Salpiglossis	A	S. sinuata	multi-coloured, veined crimson, scarlet, orange, yellow	funnel-shaped; good for 'vases'
Tulip	Bb	Tulipa and varieties	red, cream, yellow, pink, striped	use single and double; can be bisected for pressing

VI Leaves

Name	Variety		Colour	Notes
Acer	Sh	varieties	red, purple	D palmate
Alchemilla	P	A. alpina	pale green, silver	D palmate, reverse silver
Amelanchier	Sh	A. canadensis	red	D autumn colour
Artemisia	P	varieties	light grey	D feathery
Dianthus	P	varieties	grey	E linear
Clematis	Cl	C. montana	dark bronze	D young leaves and fluffy seed heads
Eccremocarpus	Cl	E. scaber	brown	
Elaeagnus	Sh	E. pungens	green, gold	E ovate leathery; splashed with gold
Escallonia	Sh	E. macrantha	dark green	E small glossy ovate
Euonymus	Sh	E. japonicus	variegated	E glossy ovate
Ivy	Cl	Hedera 'Marginata' and varieties	cream edged	E sprays, single leaves
Jasmine	Cl	Jasminum officinale	green	D pinnate
Potentilla	W	P. anserina (silver weed)	grey, silver	D toothed leaves in leaflets; use whole or leaflets

Name	Variety		Colour	Notes
Poplar	*T*	*Populus alba*	grey, green	*D* reverse side white
Rhus	*T*	*R. typhina* (sumach)	orange, purple	*D* pinnate, autumn colo
Rose	*Sh*	*varieties*	green, gold, yellow	*D* autumn colour
Rosemary	*Sh*	*Rosmarinus officinalis*	grey	*E* small linear white on reverse
Senecio	*A*	*S. cineraria maritima*	light grey	*E* leaves deeply lobed
	Sh	*S. laxifolius*	silver, grey	*D* ovate white on reverse
Spiraea	*Sh*	*S.x. bumalda* 'Anthony Waterer'	some pink, cream	*D* lanceolate toothed
		S.x. bumalda 'Goldflame'	orange, gold	
Tanacetum	*P*	*T. haradjanii*	silver, grey	*E* small lanceolate deeply dissected
Vine	*Cl*	*Vitis* 'Purpurea'	claret, purple	*D* five lobed grey on reverse; pick end sprays and small leaves
Willow	*T*	*Salix alba*	silver, grey	*D* narrow linear; pick when young

IV

Creating Pictures from Dried Material

23
Collecting dried material

Sometimes when introduced to strangers I am described as the lady who makes dried flower pictures. This I hasten to correct and I explain the difference between dried and pressed flowers. The main difference is that by pressing, flowers become two dimensional whilst drying retains the original three-dimensional shape of the flower; and of course the method is quite different. There are several ways of drying material, but for the purpose of this book and to make the pictures described, I use two ways only: first allowing flowers and seed heads to dry naturally with the minimum of help; and secondly by using glycerine to preserve leaves. Other ways of drying such as immersing material in silica gel, borax or other drying materials, I consider unsatisfactory for making pictures. Flowers preserved in this way need an extremely dry atmosphere to maintain their shape, which cannot be achieved unless they are hermetically sealed in their setting — this is impossible in an ordinary picture frame, however well the glass fits. Very pretty arrangements of flowers can be purchased, sometimes including butterflies placed in glass domes filled with colourful dried flowers of great variety. But underneath the dome, if you turn it over, you will see instructions telling the owner not to remove the glass that is sealed firmly onto the base. This would let in the air and so in time ruin the group.

Several kinds of everlasting flowers known by the Victorians as 'immortelles' can easily be raised in your own garden; these can be grown from seed obtainable from most garden centres, or you can find them in your seed catalogue and send for them. One of the most popular and the most colourful is the half-hardy annual heli-chrysum or straw flower (I treat it as a hardy annual), which comes in almost any colour ranging from white to cream, yellow and orange to red, and pale pink to deep crimson, and in sizes ranging from 2 cm (¾ in.) to 5 cm (2 in.). A more delicate flower to grow is the annual helipterum,

which has soft flowers of pink or white with a yellow centre. It is a daisy-shaped flower, semi-double. With more pointed petals and a stiffer flower but the same daisy shape, is the single or double xeranthemum which I use for pressing as well; it is a hardy annual and is white (my favourite) or pale or deep lilac. Easily grown and equally colourful is statice or sea lavender. All these flowers are described as everlasting, which is exactly what they are, and without any treatment, because of their straw like texture, they will always remain the same though their leaves will have dried and have to be removed.

As you see there is no limit to the range of colours you can use when making dried flower pictures; but to get variety you will need a wide range of plant material. Grasses can play a large part in adding to the mixture. Packets of mixed grass seed beloved by flower arrangers are of great value and are more spectacular than the kinds found in the fields and hedgerows. Once you have sown them they will spring up each year if you don't weed them out. I have quaking grass *Briza media* and hare's tail *Lagurus ovatus* here and there in my garden from seed sown three years ago. But don't neglect the fields and hedgerows which abound in many species of interesting grasses; also look out for seed heads to add to your collection of material for your dried pictures. Seed heads are numerous — honesty, to name one, can be used with great success. Useful also are small pine cones and the much smaller ones to be found on the alder tree.

An annual which most gardeners seem to grow is the larkspur. Though not one of the natural everlastings, nevertheless, it will dry most satisfactorily for use in your pictures. If you don't have it in your garden the florist will certainly have bunches at the appropriate time of year. Mention here should be made of the hydrangea, useful both as a pressed flower and for drying. Achillea is another useful plant of the yarrow family with flat plate-like heads, which dries naturally, as also does anaphalis, a herbaceous perennial. It has sprays of small white pom-pom type flowers, thus adding another variation to your collection.

As seed heads form during the summer and autumn, pick the ones you think might add interest to your arrangements. So often dead heads are cut off by tidy gardeners, and one does not realize how beautiful a seed head can be; so do allow some of your plants to complete their life cycle!

One of the leaves which makes a useful background to a picture is bracken. Sprays of bracken picked at different times of the year will dry in shades from light brown and bronze to yellow as the year advances. They will dry naturally but tend to curl up, so will have to be dried by gentle pressing. You do not need to own a flower press for this purpose as the leaves only have to be dried to prevent curling, and do not have to be pressed very hard. All that has to be done is to place the fronds between sheets of newspaper under a rug or mat, leave it for a week or so and the bracken will be ready for use. See the glossary on pp. 103 — 104 for some of the flowers and leaves I have found suitable for drying.

Buying dried material

For those who have no garden and perhaps are unable to venture into the fields and woods in search of suitable material to use for pictures, many florists now sell ready dried flowers and leaves. You can choose from a great variety of professionally dried and prepared material. Beware, though, of any flowers which have been dyed. These will never look natural, and there is a wide enough choice without resorting to artificially coloured ones. Pre-packing has even reached the florists where one can buy a selection of dried material beautifully packed in boxes or packets ready to be used to make complete winter arrangements. These can easily be included in your pictures. The mixture is fairly varied and the colours are carefully blended.

Nearly all florists sell everlasting flowers as they come into season. Most commonly helichrysum and statice are to be found, usually in bunches of mixed colours. Make sure that the flowers of the helichrysum are not too far out and still have their petals curled into the centre. Larkspur is worth buying when you see it; the pretty pink, blue or white sprays contrast well with the daisy shapes of helipterum, xeranthemum or helichrysum. Another member of the statice family *Limonium suworowii* is also a useful addition. It has dense spikes of rosy lilac some inches long which make another different shape.

24
How to dry materials

Natural drying

Flowers technically termed 'everlasting' need hardly any drying at all; their straw like texture contains no moisture, and when picked they retain their shape and colour permanently. The leaves and stems will dry off. The leaves should be picked or rubbed off when they have dried and become brittle. If you are going to need the stems it is advisable to put a wire through the heads of helichrysum and helipterum before hanging them to dry. Tie them up in bunches and hang them in a cool dry place. When the leaves have died off and been removed you can store them in boxes for later use. Flowers such as larkspur and achillea should be tied and hung upside down in a dry, airy and dark place. Unless dried upside down the tips of larkspur or delphinium will bend over as they dry and so spoil the shape of the spray.

Hydrangea is universally dried for winter use and yet there are always different ideas as to the best way of doing this. It probably varies with the kind of hydrangea and the conditions under which it has grown. I wait until the flowers feel slightly papery to the touch. I then pick the heads and place them in a container of water and gradually after a week or so they will have become really dry. Some shrivel up, but most dry successfully this way. A vase of hydrangeas picked and placed in the living room as an arrangement will very often after a week or so become dry and can then remain as a winter decoration. Small sprays of a dried head can be cut off and used for pictures when you need them.

Any seed heads which you may gather will probably be dry, if not, very nearly dry. Tidy them up and if they are quite dry they can be stored on their stalks in jam jars or hung up, whichever is more convenient, or put away in boxes. But wherever you store dried material it must be in a dry atmosphere. Honesty will need to have the outer husks of the seed heads rubbed off to reveal the beautiful mother-of-pearl discs underneath. I use these for pressed as well as dried flower pictures. Grasses can be placed in containers of water where they will gradually lose their green hue and take on the colour of hay as they dry off.

Before using dried material in pictures, spraying with a clear varnish aerosol will help preserve it and give a dull sheen. This is a particularly good idea with any cones you may use.

Preserving with glycerine

Striking mahogany-coloured leaves can be obtained by preserving some in glycerine. They will be rich looking and shiny and will provide you with a perfect background for some of your less delicate creations. Rhododendrons and laurel leaves acquire a beautiful leathery appearance when treated in this way. Use only leaves that are evergreen as their texture is much thicker than deciduous ones and they will retain their shape. Portuguese laurel has smaller leaves than the common laurel, and therefore can be more useful in smaller pictures. About the same size leaf as the Portuguese laurel is sweet bay. Laurustinus is another shrub with small leaves which absorbs glycerine well.

To make a solution for preserving your material use one part of glycerine to two parts of warm water. Place the mixture in a container and immerse the stems in a few inches of the solution. Let them remain until the leaves change colour which will take two to three weeks. Before placing in the glycerine trim off any foliage which will not be needed. Glycerine is quite expensive, and you do not want to preserve unnecessary leaves. After a day or so top up with warm water if required. When you remove the glycerined leaves lie them flat in a dark place to allow them to mature a bit. I have some beautiful preserved leaves which are some years old and have the appearance of and are as pliant and shiny as soft leather. Incidentally, I keep these for my winter dried flower arrangements. I dust them off and put them away each year for the following year. By placing some of the glycerined

xeranthemum

statice

helichrysum

hydrangea

anaphalis

quaking grass

65 *Flowers that dry naturally.*

leaves in bright sunlight this will have a bleaching effect which will vary the colour of your preserved leaves.

25
Frames for dried arrangements

Pictures created from dried material will need to be framed in what could be described as a shallow box with glass forming the lid. To contain the arrangement which will stand out 2½ 5 cm (1½ 2 in.) from the background, the recess of the frame must be deep enough to prevent the flowers touching the glass covering it. Picture moulding with a suitable depth can be bought from a picture-framer or art shop and can be made up for you. Deep frames will cost a little bit more, being heavier and with a wider edge to the frame. It is quite easy even if you're not a handyman to add strips of wood onto the back of the frame to give the required depth. These will need to have the corners mitred to make a perfect fit. If you have a mitre block this is not difficult and it will cost less, as the moulding you buy for the frame will be much cheaper than a heavier frame with its greater width and depth.

Backgrounds

Different coloured card makes a very suitable background for dried pictures. There is a good range of colours from which to choose. Dried flowers are fairly bright, so decide on a background which will blend with your picture and frame. You can buy card from an art shop for about £1 a sheet, and this will normally provide you with more than one background. The card is approximately 85 cm x 55 cm (34 in. x 22 in.).

Mounting board is another kind of firm card also obtainable from art shops. Some boards have woven texture and others a smooth matt surface, and the choice of colour is just as wide as that of the card. Neutral backgrounds always fit in better than vivid coloured ones. A dull gold frame with a brown background with brown and orange flowers will produce a pleasing group. A silver frame with a grey or very pale blue background with white and blue flowers makes a pretty combination. Dark green will always combine with any colour flowers.

Fabrics are also suitable for backgrounds but not such fine ones as those used for the more delicate pressed flower pictures. Linen, hessian, felt or even velvet can all be used satisfactorily.

There is an infinite number of combinations and permutations mixing flowers, frames and backgrounds. By trial and error you will achieve the arrangements which will please you most. So much, however, will depend on the kind of frames you are able to obtain, and this is really the starting point.

If, after reading the description of frames needed for this type of picture, you feel that it might be too difficult to find suitably deep frames or to make them deep enough yourself, try making a picture in an ordinary frame with a background of card or mounting board described, but without the glass. For this picture, a fairly narrow moulding, and therefore an inexpensive one, is all that is needed. The background card should be cut to fit onto the back of the frame. This should be stuck on. The back can then be finished by gluing down a similar sized piece of backing paper. For a firmer finish or a heavier picture, nail a piece of hardboard onto the back before finally sticking on the backing paper. This operation will have to be completed before making the picture itself as once the flowers have been stuck in place you will not be able to reverse the whole picture to stick on or nail down the backing as the flowers will protrude an inch or so outside the frame.

There is no reason why you should not make some very attractive pictures using this method, but they will not be such lasting pictures and will have to be hung well out of reach of any possibility of being knocked, which might cause some of the brittle flowers to fall off. Dust is another hazard but a good blow every so often will help to disperse this. It is also possible to make an arrangement by using only a piece of hardboard which you have covered with hessian or linen, and so dispensing with the frame altogether. This type of 'plaque' can look very attractive in the right setting, and making it might be good practice before embarking on a more ambitious work.

26
Making the picture

Equipment

- Frame
- Card for the background and sides of the frame
- Hardboard for the backing
- Fabric (if used) for the background and sides of the frame
- Glass
- Small paint brush
- Stanley knife (10-601)
- Tweezers
- Ruler
- Adhesive
- Paper for backing the frame
- Panel pins
- Scissors
- Clear varnish aerosol spray
- Screw eyes
- Wire or string

Preparing the background

When you make a picture of any type, it is easier if the frame is in place when arranging the material. By doing this the complete work can be assessed and can be altered, added to or pieces taken out, and more importantly, arranged in the correct position in relation to the frame. For this kind of picture the frame must actually rest on the background. Measure the outside of the frame and using a ruler as a guide score along the card with the Stanley knife. A sharp knife should cut right through the card, but be careful that you don't cut the surface underneath. I use a thin piece of plyboard on my work table. If you have bought the card from art suppliers you could save yourself some trouble by asking to have it cut with the guillotine that will be part of the equipment of any frame-makers' shop. They will probably have supplied the frame as well, so this should be easy. They will also fix the glass in for you. For the picture framer this is a simple matter

as nowadays glass is set into the frame with a glazing point driver and it is done in a matter of seconds. If you have had the glass put in for you and so are unable to make your picture with the frame in place, make a mock-up by using four pieces of card cut to the correct size of the frame which you can then place on the background. This will give you enough guidance.

If you are using a fabric background, this can be stuck directly onto a piece of hardboard cut to the size of the outside of the frame. Cut the fabric the same size and stick it firmly onto the smooth side of the hardboard. The fabric must adhere all over the surface of the hardboard so that there will be no bubbles in the cloth. Leave enough fabric over to cut strips to stick onto the inner sides of the frame to finish later. If the fabric used is inclined to fray, iron it onto a piece of fine 'iron-on' interfacing before cutting.

Arranging the material

Have a piece of card or paper the size of the background, select the material you need for your picture and arrange it on this with the mock-up frame round it. When you are satisfied that this is how you want your picture, and only then, start sticking the pieces onto the background. Beginning with the outside, each piece must be transferred in turn and stuck down. If you are not confident that you can rearrange the material in exactly the same way before starting to stick, use a ruler and measure the distances of some of the pieces from the edge of the frame and mark their position on the background with a pencil. With this to guide you the pieces should soon fall into position. Make certain that none of the flower heads stick up high enough to touch the glass.

If, for example, you are using small pine cones, in order to make them stick more firmly they can be wired with florist's wire and inserted into a small piece of plasticine which has been stuck

4 Colourful mixed flowers make up this large arrangement representing a 'Dutch' flower piece.

5 A mixed bunch of flowers in paper collage. A flamboyant striped tulip dominates the arrangement. Grouped below are a passion flower, some auriculas and a spray of forget-me-not. Balancing the right hand side is a small gaillardia and bud.

6 An arrangement of dried leaves, grasses and seed heads. The picture has been placed in a shallow frame without glass.

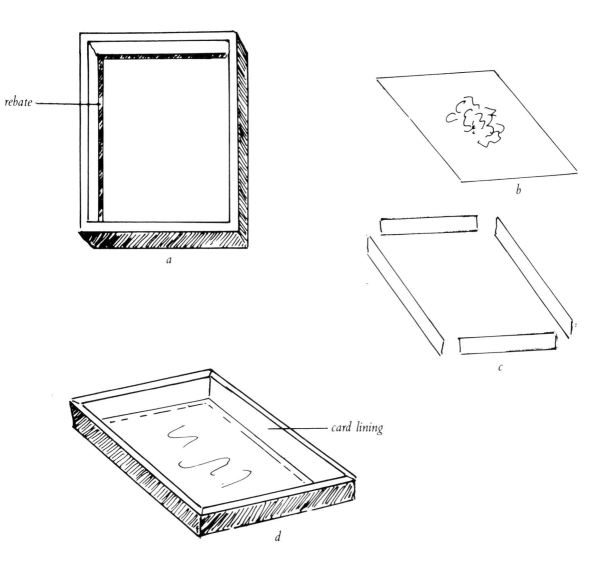

66 Fixing the glass into a box frame: (a) frame reversed showing rebate; (b) card for the background cut to fit the back of the frame; (c) strips of card for innerside of frame cut 1½ cm (⅝ in.) narrower than the side to allow for thickness of glass; (d) frame face down with glass resting on rebate. The card lining side (c) hold it in place.

onto the background. A piece about 4-5 cm (1½-2 in.) moulded into a small mound 2 cm (¾ in.) high will be adequate. Use an adhesive which will give a strong bond such as Araldite to attach the Plasticine, and for additional strength smear some onto the pine cones before placing them in the plasticine.

Finishing a picture with glass

If the glass has not been fixed by the frame supplier, you will now have to do this yourself (*fig. 66*). The glass will be held in place by the card forming the inner sides of the frame, or if fabric has been used, by the card covered by the fabric. Clean the glass thoroughly, lie the frame face down and place the glass in it. It will rest against the rebate (a). Measure the sides and cut strips of the same card (b) as that used for the background (c) exactly to fit the inner sides of the frame but allowing for the depth of the glass which will be about 1½ mm (¹/₁₆ in.). Stick these four pieces firmly onto the inner sides of the frames and the thickness of the card will hold the glass in place (d).

The frame is now ready to place over the arrangement. Remove all stray bits and specks from your picture and make sure that everything is firmly stuck down. If you give it a shake and turn it upside down you will very soon find out if this is not so. Reverse the frame and run a line of adhesive using plenty, all round the moulding so

that it is well covered — a finger is the best to for spreading — and then turn the picture ov and press it firmly onto the frame. Place a hea book on the back to weigh it down and so ensur good join. After this, nail on the hardboard w panel pins or stick on another layer of card a finish with backing paper. By finishing in t way you have a much neater and more so picture. Add the screw eyes and wire and yo picture is ready for hanging. I like the back o picture to look as well finished as the front. your background is of fabric stuck onto hardboa a thin piece of card or backing paper will enough to achieve the desired result.

Finishing a picture without glass

As is explained on p. 91 the back of this picture finished before you actually start making t arrangement. The card is cut to the size of t back of the frame and stuck on. A piece of card hardboard cut the same size is added. If you us second piece of card, sticking will be enough t hardboard needs nailing using panel pins. Fina stick on the backing paper. Make holes for screw eyes so that they can easily be screwed and the picture wire or string fitted when picture is finished.

If the background is of fabric it must be stu onto a piece of hardboard, cut exactly the size the outside edge of the frame. This is then stuck nailed onto the back and finished as describe

27
Designs for pictures

A posy of flowers (fig. 67)

The picture in fig. 68 is made on a piece of pale blue mounting board 25.5 cm x 20 cm (10 in. x 8 in.). The insides of the frame have been lined with the same card as that used for the background. The depth of the frame is 2.5 cm (1 in.). Make the outline first by placing the longest spray of blue

67 *A posy of flowers.*

larspur in the centre. To give width two pieces of *Statice suworowii* are placed lower down on each side. Note that the pieces of statice, although they are arranged so that they are equidistant from the edge of the background, are not similar enough to make the outline look stiff. One has a slight bend as it curls downwards. These three pieces can safely be stuck down before placing the remaining material.

Next a shorter spray of blue larkspur is arranged on the right of centre. In this picture each floret of larkspur has been stuck on separately, and similarly on the left side florets of pink larkspur are added to resemble a spray. Fine, assorted stalks of differing lengths are now placed in the centre of the picture to give a good overall shape and balance to the arrangement (a). These can be stuck down. Two stems of seedheads of flax are placed next on either side of the right-hand larkspur spray. The gaps are now filled in with florets of yellow *Statice sinuatum*, stuck separately, and then sprays of grass (in this picture creeping bent grass) and sea lavender, *Statice vulgare*, are stuck on both sides to meet the top of the stems. These are concealed by two open pink helipterum and three buds in gradated sizes with honesty, hydrangea and a small head of yellow lonas to complete the arrangement (b). The picture is now ready for the frame to be fixed in place.

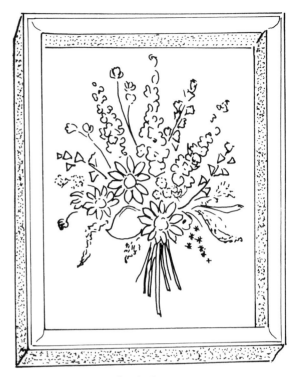

finished picture

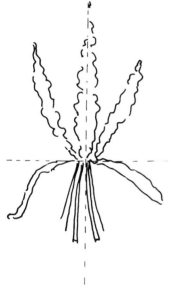

outline of arrangement

68 A posy of flowers.

completing the arrangement

69 An arrangement using seed heads, leaves and pine cones.

Picture without flowers (fig. 69)

The picture illustrated in fig. 69 has been placed in a frame, but without glass. The outside of the frame measures 38 cm x 28 cm (15 in. x 11 in.) and the depth 1 cm (½ in.). The mount has been nailed onto the back of the frame, and has been finished with a piece of backing paper stuck onto the back of the card. Holes have been made to take the screw eyes when the arrangement has been completed and the picture is ready for hanging. Before sticking the card onto the frame, the sides have been lined with the same card which was used for the background.

As this is an arrangement using fairly heavy materials, a piece of Plasticine, 5 cm (2 in.) in circumference and 2.5 cm (1 in.) high has been stuck, using araldite, in the centre of the background. This will enable some of the material to be wired and stuck into the Plasticine. The pine cones, the seed heads and the bracken were sprayed with a clear aerosol varnish before use. First the outline is suggested by bracken and fern fronds and five small, glycerined rhododendron leaves. These have all been stuck onto the background round the Plasticine (a). A spray of glycerined seed heads of deutzia is pushed into

70 Different methods of attaching wire to floral material.

the Plasticine at the top on the left side, while two seed heads of love-in-the-mist, just off centre, dominate the top, balanced by a spray of dried seed heads of annual lavatera. The arrangement is filled in with more seed heads of lavatera, a spray of hare's tail grass, three clusters of ivy berries, two sprays of yellow tansy, a stem of silver honesty pods and sprays of *Sisyrinchium bermudiana*

97

71 *Construction of the design: (a) step 1; (b) step 2; (c) step 3.*

1 *fronds of bracken and fern;* **2** *rhododendron leaves;* **3** *deutzia;* **4** *seedheads;* **5** *love-in-the-mist;* **6** *spray of lavatera seedheads;* **7** *hare's tail grass;* **8** *ivy berries;* **9** *tansy;* **10** *honesty seed discs;* **11** Sisyrinchium bermudiana; **12** *pine cones.*

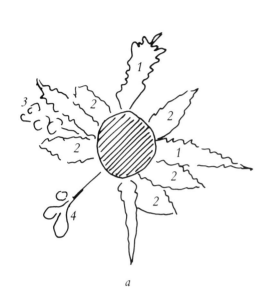

a

b

c

d flax seed heads. As all these have hard stems
·y were easy to insert into the Plasticine. The
·angement was completed by the addition of a
·v more rhododendron leaves and three pine
·nes all of which were wired and inserted into
· Plasticine (c).

To wire pine cones, take a piece of florist's
·re, double it and hook it half way up the cone
·o the scales bringing the two ends down to the
·se on the opposite side, twist tightly together to
·ke a stem (*fig. 70*). To wire leaves, thread a
·ce of florist's wire through the back of the leaf
·quarter to a third of the way up, join the two
·ds together and twist to make a stem (*fig. 70*).

Circular design on a square base (fig. 72)

This arrangement fits into a frame 18 cm (7 in.)
square and 2 cm (¾ in.) deep after the glass has
been inserted. The colour scheme is basically
white, with the addition of a few yellow lonas
heads. The background is medium grey card, and
the insides of the frame have been lined with the
same card. The frame itself, though a wooden
one, has the appearance of dull silver which

*72 Dried flowers make up this very simple circular design.
Honesty discs and helipterum are the main ingredients of
the picture.*

complements and tones with the arrangement. This design is circular and would do equally well for a square or round frame and the group measures approximately 10 cm (4 in.) square. To define the shape of the group, the silvery discs of five honesty seed heads are first stuck down to form a rough circle; the two on the horizontal line are equidistant from the outside edges (a). This simple arrangement is then filled between the honesty discs with seed heads of flax, small pieces of the feathery seed heads of clematis, sea

lavender, quaking grass and some florets of *St* *sinatum*. Two heads of tansy and three of Ionas added to emphasize the yellow centres of white helipterum, which are added last which will conceal any stems which meet in centre (b).

73 A circular design. (a) forming the shape of arrangement; (b) finishing the design; (c) the arrangen completed.

a

b

c

28
Glass domes

In no way can arrangements in glass domes be described as pictures, which is what this book is all about. Arrangements of dried flowers that are invaluable in the winter when fresh ones are scarce, will be removed when spring comes to make way for fresh flowers. But a glass dome filled with dried flowers will look attractive on a table or shelf at any time of the year, and in fact becomes part of the furnishings of the room like a porcelain figure. Thus my reason for including them in this book. I have had a dome in my sitting room for the last ten years and it always gives me pleasure to look at it and of course the contents never get dusty. The sealed glass domes mentioned earlier have flowers in them which have been dried with desiccants and which depend on air-tight conditions to keep their shape.

The domes I describe here are filled with material which has dried naturally, either on the plant or by hanging up, or by absorbing glycerine, and so will not need to be kept in air-tight conditions. Domes, either plastic or glass, which are manufactured primarily to cover clocks can be obtained through a jeweller or watch- and clock-maker, or direct from suppliers of watch and clock parts. Sizes range from quite small, about 7 cm (3 in.) in height, and prices range from approximately £5. It is also possible to find oval or round glass domes in antique shops. These will almost certainly be Victorian. Often they will have stuffed birds in them and even groups of butterflies, but you may be lucky and come across one which has nothing in it. Some years ago I bought an oval dome in an antique shop about 20 cm (8 in.) high containing two very small stuffed birds perched on a branch set into a rock with tufts of dried grass growing out of it. It was so pretty I could not bring myself to dismantle it to use for dried flowers, which had been my intention, so the birds are still in the dome perched together on their branch. Another time I bought a much bigger dome with a large bouquet of flowers beautifully made with different coloured wools. This I did use, hoping my dried flowers would look prettier than the woollen ones. They did!

Domes which you buy from a watch-maker will need a wooden base on which to rest, though if bought from an antique dealer will probably be complete — if not you should pay very much less. If needed, the wooden base can be made for you quite easily by a wood turner, but take the dome to him so that he can see that the top fits perfectly onto the base. Usually it fits into a slot cut just inside the rim.

Filling a glass dome

To make a foundation in which to insert the dried flowers I have found a lump of plasticine the most satisfactory. Plasticine when warm is fairly soft. A small piece about the size of half an egg should be enough for a dome with a base about 13 cm (5 in.). Put the Plasticine in a warm place, even on a hot radiator, until it is really warm and pliable, then mould it into a small domed shape about 5 cm (2 in.) across and 3 cm (1½ in.) high. To make sure it will stay firmly stuck in place put a blob of clear adhesive on the base and press the Plasticine onto it. While the Plasticine is still soft stalks of material can be inserted much more easily. It may be necessary to wire some of the flowers in order to fix them into the base, and fine stems may have to be wired together.

In arranging your flowers always work from the top down towards the base of the dome. Start with the spiky material, the tallest piece of which must be at least 1 cm (½ in.) from the top of the dome. See that none of your material overhangs flowers lower down. Aim at an overall conical shape. To achieve this, as you make up your arrangement keep turning the base round to ensure that the arrangement can be viewed from all angles. It should be reasonably symmetrical

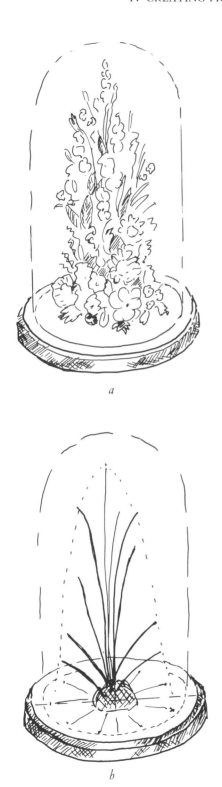

but not too stiff. You can prevent this by varying the material you use. Try to fill the arrangement completely as you work downwards. Remember that it is not easy to add pieces where you may have left gaps. The material is very dry and brittle and inserting pieces amongst material already arranged can easily cause some nicely-placed flower heads to snap off. Also remember that as you work downwards the length of the material gets shorter! Wiring will help, as wire ends can often be more easily inserted into the Plasticine than stalks or stems. The finished arrangement should be no nearer the glass at the base than 1 cm (½ in.) and should be equidistant all round.

The dome illustrated in fig. 74 is 25.5 cm (10 in.) high and 14 cm (5½ in.) wide and is resting in a slot in the base which is 16 cm (6½ in.) in diameter. It has been filled with a colourful variety of naturally dried flowers. Starting at the top there are sprays of lavender, quaking grass, sprays of pink and dark blue larkspur and one spray of *Statice suworowii*. The stems of none of these have been wired as it was easy to push them into the so far empty mound of Plasticine. Revolving downwards, shorter sprays of quaking grass have been repeated, some yellow heads of tansy, a pink helichrysum and a white helipterum flower (both wired) have been inserted and as the dome is turned *Statice sinatum*, sea lavender, more helichrysum and alchemilla added. Nearing the base there are clusters of sulphur-coloured santolina, purple statice, deep crimson, pink and yellow heads of helichrysum all of which have been wired, and a head of golden achillea. Sprays of anaphalis have been wired together and stuck in bunches into the base of the arrangement alternating with small heads of green hydrangea and more sprays of statice.

The arrangement is very colourful and protected by its dome could well become an antique of the future!

a

b

74 (a) *Dried flowers in a glass dome; (b) shows the material radiating outwards and upwards from the Plasticine.*

29

Table of flowers for preserving

bbreviations

Annual
Bulb
Climber
Flower
Leaf
Perennial
Seed head
Shrub

owers leaves and seed heads for preserving

me		Variety	Description (colour of leaf described after preserving)	Method of preserving
chemilla	P	A. mollis	F lime green tiny flowers in clusters	air dry
nmobium	A	A. alatum grandiflorum	F white daisy-type, yellow centre	air dry
aphalis (arl everlasting)	P	A. triplinervis	{ F small white flower sprays	air dry
		A. margaritacea		
y	Sh	Laurus nobilis	L bronze	place in glycerine
matis	Cl	varieties	S feathery silver	pick when seed heads just formed; place in glycerine or leave on plant to dry naturally
detia	A	G. grandiflora	S head of small pea-like pods	cut when dry; if left some will self seed
mphrena	A	G. globosa	F orange, yellow, purple, pink, ovoid flower heads	air dry; cut before flowers are fully out
ape hyacinth	Bb	Muscari armeniacum	S silver small circular capsules on stem	leave to dry on plant
psophila	P	various	F tiny white flowers on sprays	air dry
lichrysum (raw flower)	A	H. bracteatum	{ F red, pink, yellow orange, cream, white	air dry
	P	H. bellidioides	F white, small	cut before fully open

Name		Variety	Description	Method of preserving
Helipterum (Rhodanthe)	A	H. manglesii	F pink, white daisy-shape yellow centre	air dry; cut before fully open
Honesty	B	Lunaria annua	S silver discs	dry on plant
Hydrangea	Sh	varieties	F blue, pink, white	cut when flower head feel papery
Ivy	Cl	Hedera varieties	L brown	place in glycerine
Larkspur	A	Delfinium ajacis	F pink, blue, white	cut when buds on top sprays are still unopened; air dry
Laurel (common) (Portugal)	Sh	Prunus laurocerasus P. lusitanica	L bronze L bronze	place in glycerine single leaves or sprays
Lonas	A	L. annua	F clusters of golden heads	air dry
Moluccella (bells of Ireland)	A	M. Laevis	F lime green, turns nearly white	remove leaves; air dry or place in glycerine
Nigella (love-in-a-mist)	A	N. damascena	S green, blue	air dry
Poppy	A	Papaver rhoeas	S light brown	air dry
Rhodanthe	A	see Helipterum		
Rhododendron	Sh	various	L dark brown	glycerine; use smaller leaves; can be sun bleached
Santolina	Sh	various	F deep ochre flower heads	allow to dry on plant
Statice	A	Limonium sinuatum L. suworowii	F pink, yellow, white, purple sprays F rose pink spikes	cut before flowers fully open
Tansy	W	Tanacetum vulgare	F golden button-shaped flowers	allow to dry on plant
Xeranthemum	A	X. annum	F pink lilac on white crisp satin-like petals; daisy shape	pick before fully open

V

Cards and Calendars

30
Cards

A hand-made card for an anniversary is most welcome and much more appreciated than one you may have purchased. The card need not necessarily be an elaborate work which has taken a lot of time to make. A perfect pressed specimen of a flower with an accompanying leaf can look just as pretty as a more detailed arrangement. The fact that you have thought out a design and executed it yourself can give great pleasure to the recipient. In fact such a person may well go so far as to frame your offering.

The most important wedding anniversaries are particularly easy to make cards for because of the colours associated with them, silver for 25 years, ruby for 40 years and gold for 50 years. Figure 75a shows the card I have made for a Golden Wedding anniversary using pressed flowers. The background was cut from a good quality, buff

75 Greetings cards and a calendar. The calendar had been made with pressed leaves and is heat-sealed. Three of the cards are of pressed flowers and covered with transparent adhesive plastic. The card in the right-hand corner is a paper collage — the irises and primroses are in silhouette cut from black card.

a

b

c

d

76 Greetings cards. (a) An anniversary card using flowers. (b) Red roses of paper make a suitable card for a Ruby Wedding. (c) A simple design in paper collage, of daisies with twinning stems. (d) Tiny pressed flowers are used for this more elaborate card.

gres paper (art shops supply this in many
lours) which is thick enough to fold and stand
right. The card measures approximately 17½ cm
2½ cm (7 in. x 5 in.). A gold line was drawn 1
(½ in.) inside the edge, and the arrangement
s placed at the bottom right hand corner.
rays of mimosa were used to mark the outline.
ttercups and potentilla flowers formed the
se with the addition of cowslip heads and
cken leaflets, the dark contrast being obtained
the use of *Clematis montana* leaves.

A Ruby Wedding anniversary could well be
picted by the paper collage rose tree (*fig. 75b*).
is was made on white Waterman paper. This
o has a gold border round the edge. The tree
s a coyly curved trunk with two branches off
main stem and the leaves were cut from two
ades of green. The roses were made by cutting
all circles of red tissue paper, about 2.5 cm
in.)in diameter, which were then screwed up
d shaped with the fingers to the size required.
vo of the roses have double circles, one pink
d one red. Dabs of adhesive were put where the
ses were to be placed and they were pressed
ry firmly into position. The card was finished
th some paper cut to resemble blades of grass
d stuck at the foot of the tree. This card can be
de very quickly and from it it is possible to
olve ideas for other simple designs in the same
le. A flower pot with geraniums or a group of
ocuses would be equally effective.

More elaborate cards will take longer to put
gether, but if you have a collection of small

flowers you can make some very attractive
miniature pictures. The card (*fig. 75c*) is on a
green background on which has been stuck a
piece of white paper to form a mount. A gold line
has been drawn 1 cm (½ in.) inside the edge of the
card and another line on the inside edge of the
white mount. All this helps to give a good finish.
A small arrangement has been made in the centre.
The main flower is a deep crimson potentilla
surrounded by a primrose, magenta, lobelia,
feverfew, a tiny blue hydrangea, two veratrum
flowers and a small spray of orange lewisia,
feathery leaves forming the outline. As this is a
fairly elaborate group, containing a quantity of
material, it has been covered with clear plastic
for protection. (This is usually used as an outer
transparent cover for the paper jackets of books
and can be bought at bookshops or stationers in
rolls.)

A simple design for daisies for a greetings card
(*fig. 76d*) is treated in a decorative manner from an
Art Nouveau design characterized by the entwin-
ing of the stems. The petals of the daisies are made
up of a mixture of white tissue paper and an
opaque white matt paper. The leaves and stems
are blue green, lighter than the grey blue
background on which the flowers are stuck. A
double line has been drawn round the card which
is mounted on a larger piece of the same colour.
This also has a line drawn just inside the edges.
Lemon-coloured centres make an interesting
addition of colour and are softer than the
traditional orange.

31
Calendars

ie calendar in the left corner of fig. 76 is made
pressed leaves with a few buds which have
en mounted on a heavy piece of cream board.
r protection the board has been heat sealed and
en mounted on a further piece of board, this
ne in olive green. As a finish a gold line has been

drawn 5 mm (¼ in.) inside the edges. A curling
stem of ivy has been arranged at the top left,
counterbalanced by a heavy bronze *Clematis
montana* leaf, above which is a spray of buds of
Rosa rubrafolium. Opposite is a twisting stem of
Clematis montana leaves. Five star-like flowers of

veratrum fall from below the leaves while a mass of delicate elder buds is placed on the right above the rose buds. There is a beautiful bronze rose leaf showing sharply serrated edges next to the ivy. The centre of the arrangement, on which all the stems converge, is filled with ivy, montana, one red maple leaf, a silver *Alchemilla alpina* leaf reversed and two silver honesty seed husks.

77 A paper collage calendar. A collection of spring flowers: tulips, daffodils, narcissi, crocus and primulas are used for this design.

The second calendar (*fig. 77*) has been prepared in the same way, a cream card mounted on a green board, lines of gold again being drawn round all the edges. This calendar is made in paper collage, depicting a group of spring flowers, cut as simply as possible, the daffodils in two shades of orange and the narcissi with yellow petals and orange centres. The larger tulip has six petals using three different reds but all taken from the same page of colour. Two shades of mauve were used for the primroses and three for the crocuses, but again all mauve shades came from the same page. Four shades of green were used. The group is easy to make as the shapes to be cut are very

78 A noticeboard. Lilies of the valley made in pape collage are used to make an attractive Art Nouveau-sty design.

simple and the design can readily be copied. Fc protection the finished work was heat sealed.

I have also included a 'notice board' (*fig. 78* This board is intended to last some time as th lilies of the valley overlap part of the paper o which the notice is to be written and therefor the paper cannot be exactly replaced although smaller piece could be substituted. The design based on Art Nouveau — a period of curved lin — and expresses the graceful movement c flowers with delicate intertwining tendrils. Th lilies are boldly portrayed, in three shades of lila with the leaves in two shades of green curvin gently upwards.

Heat sealing and clear adhesive plastic

Heat sealing, used for both of the two calendars, is a process which applies, by heat, a film of plastic onto the surface of a print or picture and so eliminates the need for a glass covering. Heat sealing will cause warping if the card is too thin, so this process is unsuitable for use on greetings cards. But prints and pictures will be held rigid by the support of the frame. Pressed material or paper collage must be well stuck down before being treated to prevent static movement during sealing. Some picture framers have a heat sealing machine and can carry out this process.

Clear adhesive plastic (such as Transpaseal) provides an excellent protection for cards, calendars and anything else that is not covered by glass; it is easy to apply if the directions are carefully followed.

List of suppliers

Dried flowers:
Winterflora
Hall Farm
Weston
Beccles
Suffolk
NR34 8TT

Frame-makers and heat-sealing specialists:
Deben Gallery
Woodbridge
Suffolk
IP12 4LU

Glass and perspex domes:
H. Walsh and Sons Ltd
243 Beckenham Road
Beckenham
Kent
BR3 4TS

Greetings cards and calendars for pressed flower
decoration:
Impress Cards
Slough Farm
Westhall
Suffolk
IP19 8RN

Bibliography

Martin, W Keble, *Concise British flora in colour*, Michael Joseph and Ebury Press, London, 1965

May, Roy and Synge, Patrick M, *Dictionary of garden plants in colour*, Michael Joseph and Ebury Press (in collaboration with the Royal Horticultural Society), London, 1969

Leymarie Jean, *Dutch paintings*, Stira, 1956

Reader's Digest Nature Lovers Library, *Field guide to the wild flowers of Britain*, The Reader's Digest Association Limited, London, 1981

Edited by Geoffrey Holme, *Flower and still life painting*, The Studio Limited, London, 1928

Readers Digest Encyclopedia of *Garden plants and flowers*, Reader's Digest Association Limited, London, 1978

Ruth Hayden, *Mrs Delany, her life and her flowers*, British Museum Publications Limited, London, 1980

Martyn Rix, *The art of the botanist*, Lutterworth Press, Guildford, 1981

Index